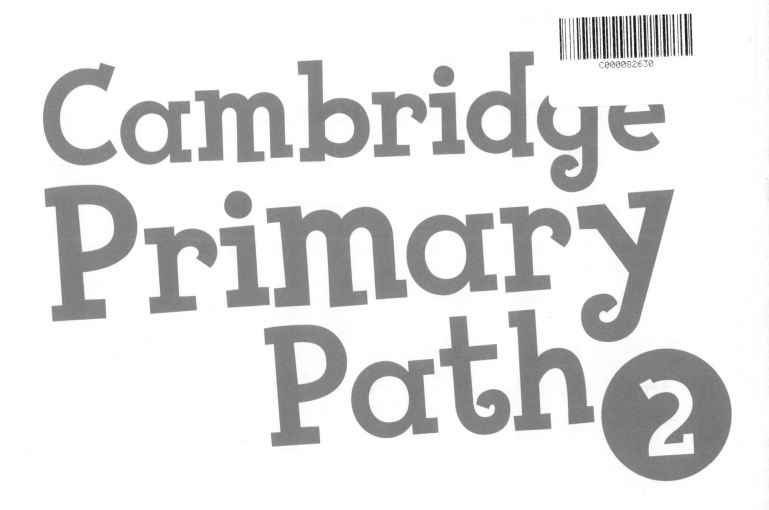

Cambridge Primary Path 2

Activity Book

Martha Fernández López

CAMBRIDGE UNIVERSITY PRESS

What is in my neighborhood?

① ▶ 1.1 **Watch the video. Complete the graphic organizer.**

firefighter ~~fire station~~ hospital doctor train station conductor

Place

| <u>fire station</u> | | |

 a

 b

 c

Person

② Key Words 1 **Complete the sentences.**

 a

There are trucks in a <u>fire station</u>.

 b

A _____ uses a hose and ladder.

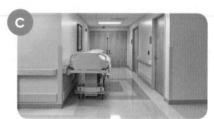 c

A doctor works at a _____.

 d

_____ and nurses help us when we are sick.

 e

Many people take a train at the _____.

 f

That's the _____ on the train.

1 Key Words 2 Complete the words and number the pictures.

1 s e c u r i t y g u a r d
2 w __ x
3 m __ s __ u __
4 j __ b

5 a __ a r m
6 f __ a __ __ l __ g h t
7 e x h __ b __ t

a  b  c  d

e  f  g  1

2 Complete the sentences with words from Activity I.

Can you guess Luke's job?

Luke has an interesting 1_____job_____.
He works in a 2_____. There,
he takes care of an important
3_____. It's a big sculpture
made of 4_____. Luke uses a
5_____ to light the museum
halls at night. Then, he sits on a chair
next to the fire 6_____. Luke
likes being a 7_____ at the
wax museum.

Reading Strategy: Headings

Headings divide the text into sections. They tell us what each section is about.

(1) **Read the text and circle the headings.**

Jobs in My Neighborhood

These are some people in my neighborhood. Their jobs are important because they make our neighborhood a better place.

A Green Job

Alan and Yamir are gardeners in my neighborhood. They take care of plants. They work in the park in front of the hospital on Mondays and Fridays. They water the plants and sometimes plant new trees, too.

Working at School

Miss Clark is a teacher. She works at my school. She teaches us writing in the morning. She likes reading us stories, and she sometimes eats with us at lunchtime.

A Job to Help Animals

I like Ivan's job. He's a vet. He takes care of animals. When your pets are sick, take them to Ivan. He can help them.

(2) **Match the headings with the sentences.**

Our Visit to the Museum	It costs five dollars on Saturdays for children. On Sundays, it is only three dollars.
An Exhibit in the Museum	I love this picture. It is a colorful painting of a house by a pond.
My Museum Ticket	In the first room, we see some paintings. Then, we look at some sculptures.

3 Read the text again and circle the correct words.

a Alan and Yamir are **teachers** / **gardeners**.

b They sometimes **plant** / **water** new trees.

c The park is **in front of** / **behind** the hospital.

d Miss Clark is a **music** / **writing** teacher.

e She works in a **hospital** / **school**.

f Ivan takes care of **animals** / **plants**.

g He can help your **plants** / **pets**.

4 Read and write the correct number.

Alan and Yamir = 1   Miss Clark = 2   Ivan = 3

a _____ works with children.

b _____ can name different kinds of flowers.

c _____ can help a sick cow.

d _____ uses books and notebooks.

e _____ knows about medicine.

5 Read and circle the correct headings.

A Nurse's Day   **A Teacher's Day**

a Today is a busy day for Rose. She is taking care of three sick people. She helps them to feel better.

At the Flower Shop   **At the Bakery**

b My parents and I are buying some cupcakes. They are on that plate. They look delicious!

At the Train Station   **At the Fire Station**

c The conductor is collecting our tickets. Now we are sitting down and are ready to go!

Prepositions of Time: *in, on, at*

at **two o'clock**, at **five o'clock**, at **II:30**

in **the morning**, in **September**, in **the evening**, in **October**

on **Monday**, on **Wednesday**, on **Sunday**

WAX MUSEUM

From 10 a.m. to 6 p.m.
Open from
Tuesday to Sunday
New exhibits: March
Guided visit: afternoon

1 **Look and match.**

1 The Wax Museum opens at   a March.

2 It closes at   b ten o'clock.

3 You can't visit the museum on   c the afternoon.

4 There are new exhibits in   d six o'clock.

5 You can have a guided visit in   e Monday.

2 **Look and mark ✓ the correct sentences.**

a	b	c	d
The bakery opens at 8 a.m. ✓	Lu works there in the evening. ☐	Cookies are three dollars on Mondays. ☐	Big cakes are seven dollars in March. ☐
The bakery opens in the evening. ☐	Lu works there in the afternoon. ☐	Cookies are three dollars on Fridays. ☐	Big cakes are seven dollars in May. ☐

(3) Complete the sentences with *in*, *on* or *at*.

a I am a student. I start school 1 _at_ eight o'clock. I play soccer
2_____ Sundays. January is my favorite month. My birthday is
3_____ January. Let's meet other people in my neighborhood!

b Jacob is a security guard. He starts work 4_____ eight o'clock and
finishes 5_____ the evening. Jacob doesn't work 6_____ Fridays.

c Sonia is a doctor and works in a hospital. She gets to the hospital
7_____ seven o'clock. She greets her patients 8_____ the morning
and then goes to her office. She works hard all year, but she
takes a break 9_____ December.

(4) Look and complete the sentences.

10:35   Thursday   ~~the morning~~   September

a He reads at
the library in
the morning .

b We take the train
at _____ .

c I see the doctor
in _____ .

d The music teacher
comes on
_____ .

My Life

Write about yourself. Use *in*, *on*, or *at*.

What time do you start school?

I start school _____ .

When is your favorite class?

My favorite class is _____ .

When do you do your homework?

I do my homework _____ .

1 Read and circle the words with the long *a* sound.

(May,) the (Baker)

I play with May
On this rainy day.
We like to bake
A big round cake.

May is late.
I have to wait
For us to bake
That big round cake.

2 Cross out the word with a different vowel sound.

a May   say   bake   ~~vet~~

b late   Jake   set   take

c bird   wake   rain   day

d play   see   wait   lake

3 Circle the words that complete the rhymes.

a When's your birthday?
Is it in (May) / March?

b Look at Jake!
What will he **buy** / **take**?

c I'll wash my plate
If it isn't too **small** / **late**!

1 Match the boxes.

Give   Don't   Ask   Take

interrupt.   turns.   your opinion.   questions.

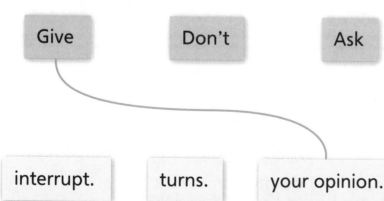

8

1A

Improve Your Writing: Compound Nouns

A compound noun has two or more nouns. There are three kinds:

1 Compound nouns with one word: **butterfly**, **birdhouse**

2 Compound nouns with two words: **fire station**, **bus stop**

3 Compound nouns with a hyphen: **great-grandfather**, **forty-five**

1 **Read and circle the compound nouns.**

There is a great museum in my neighborhood. I go there on the (weekend) with my great-grandfather. The museum has lots of interesting exhibits. There are colorful butterflies and birds. The dinosaur exhibit is amazing! We ride the bus to the museum. We know the bus driver. We know the security guard at the museum, too. He's very nice. The museum is my favorite place!

2 **Read and complete the sentences.**

> bus stop   security guard   ~~fire station~~
> train station   firefighters   police station

There are a lot of important places in my neighborhood. There is a
1 ___fire station___ that has 12
2 _____. There is also a new
3 _____. Lots of police work there. There is an old bank, and Ms. Borges is the 4_____ there.
The 5_____ is near the bank. I wait for my school bus there. My favorite place in the neighborhood is the
6_____. The trains are big and new!

Writing

1 READ Read the descriptive paragraph from SB page 15. Write the words.

a My ___favorite___ place is the park near my house.

(favorite) (best) (new)

b It is a _____ park.

(beautiful) (big) (small)

c In the park, there are _____ green trees.

(short) (old) (tall)

d There is a _____ playground.

(small) (big) (old)

> My favorite place is the park near my house. It is a beautiful park. In the park, there are tall, green trees. There are many birds and butterflies. There is a big playground with swings, a slide, and monkey bars. There is a small pond next to the playground.
> I play with toy sailboats there.
> It's the best park in the world!

2 PLAN What is your favorite place in your neighborhood? Complete the chart.

My Favorite Place	Things It Has	Adjectives

3 WRITE Write a descriptive paragraph about your favorite place in your neighborhood.

My favorite place in the neighborhood is _____

_____

_____

_____

4 EDIT Check ✓.

Writing Checklist

☐ I expressed my opinion in a descriptive paragraph.

☐ I used adjectives in a descriptive paragraph.

☐ I can identify compound nouns.

Ready to Read: Fiction

1 ⟨Key Words 4⟩ **Unscramble the words and label the pictures.**

a

beropshrab

_____

b

treest

_____

c

oodhneiborgh

_____

d

ytic

_____

e

armetksupre

_____

f

uiblingd

_____

2 **Use words from Activity I to complete the sentences. Then, number the picture.**

1 I live in a big _____city_____ , but my
  _____ is small.

2 There is a beautiful park on
  Apple _____ .

3 Mr. Keats cuts my hair at the _____ .

4 Mom and Dad buy food
  at the _____ .

5 There is a tall apartment
  _____ on Pond
  Avenue.

APPLE STREET

POND AVENUE

Reading Strategy: Predicting from Pictures

Pictures can help you know what the story is about.

1. Look at the pictures in the story and mark ✓ the correct prediction.
   Predictions:
   a The story is about a train station and people who travel. ☐
   b The story is about a security guard in a wax museum. ☐
   c The story is about a security guard at the barbershop. ☐

2. Read the story and check your prediction.

The Guard and the Flying Creature

Gibran gets ready for work. He likes his job at the wax museum in the neighborhood.

Gibran greets the school children at the museum in the morning.

There's a big wax bird in a birdhouse. The bird looks scary!

In the evening, Gibran closes the museum. The lights go out! Gibran takes his flashlight.

He walks around the museum exhibits. He hears a strange sound and sees a scary shadow. "It must be the wax bird!" he thinks.

Gibran looks again. "That's not the wax bird," says Gibran. "It's a pigeon!"

3 Circle *Yes* or *No*.

a Gibran is a security guard.   (Yes)   No

b He greets some school teachers in the morning.   Yes   No

c There's a wax bird in a birdhouse.   Yes   No

d The lights go out in the morning.   Yes   No

e The flying creature is a butterfly.   Yes   No

4 Read again and write the correct answers.

a Gibran works at the ___museum___ .

(museum) (supermarket) (barbershop)

b The museum opens in the _____ .

(morning) (afternoon) (evening)

c There is a wax bird in a _____ .

(bag) (birdhouse) (box)

5 Look and circle your predictions.

a The story is about a baker who makes cookies.

b The story is about a baker who makes bread.

c The story is about a baker who works at a supermarket.

a The story is about a conductor at a train station.

b The story is about a boy and his mom who travel by train.

c The story is about a boy and his dad who travel by train.

Prepositions of Place: *behind, between, in front of*

Where's the supermarket? It's behind **the park.**
Where are the trees? They're between **the library and the supermarket.**
Where are the apartments? They're in front of **the hospital.**

(1) Mark ✓ the correct sentences.

1 a ☑ The apartment building is behind the school.

  b ☐ The apartment building is next to the school.

2 a ☐ The bikes are next to the school.

  b ☐ The bikes are in front of the school.

3 a ☐ The supermarket is between the hospital and the fire station.

  b ☐ The fire station is between the hospital and the supermarket.

4 a ☐ The park is in front of the apartment building.

  b ☐ The park is next to the apartment building.

(2) Read and color the buildings.

a The supermarket is in front of the park. ✏

b The museum is next to the supermarket. ✏

c A library is next to the museum. ✏

d There's a school between the library and the hospital. ✏

e There are two big plants next to the supermarket. ✏

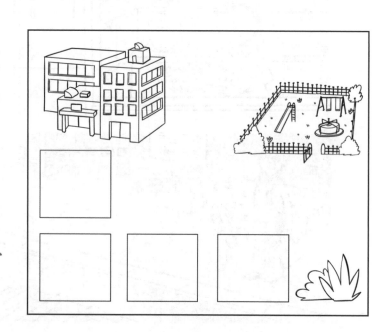

14

3 Unscramble the questions. Then, circle the answers.

Where's / hospital / the / ?

Where's the hospital?

It's in front of the park.   (It's behind the park.)

fire trucks / are / Where / the / ?

_____

They're next to the fire station.   They're behind the fire station.

the / library / Where's / ?

_____

It's behind the school.   It's between the supermarket and the school.

4 Look and complete the dialogue.

park / in front of / museum   school / behind / supermarket

a

Where's the park? _____

_____

b

_____   _____

_____   _____

My Life

Write about your neighborhood. Use prepositions of place.

a Where is your school?

My school is _____.

b Where is the park?

The park is _____.

1 Look and match.

1 Let me help you.

2 Can you repeat that, please?

3 Thank you! You're a great baker, Mom!

4 Would you like an apple?

 a

 b **1**

 c

 d

2 Color the expressions that sound polite when asking for directions.

Sure! The museum is behind the school.

Can you help me, please?

No, I won't say where the park is!

I don't want to help you!

Thank you!

Excuse me. Where's the library?

3 Draw yourself being polite to someone in your neighborhood.

Check Your Oracy!

Read and circle *Yes* or *No*.

1 I followed the ground rules for discussion.   **Yes / No**

2 I participated in the discussion.   **Yes / No**

3 I listened to my classmates.   **Yes / No**

The Big Challenge

How can we draw a map?

1 Color or 😞 .

I asked a family member to take me around the neighborhood.	
I drew a map in my notebook.	
I used my drawing to make a map on a piece of white posterboard.	
I labeled each place.	
I presented my map to the class.	

The Big Question and **Me**

Think and mark ✓. In Unit 1, I learned …

☐ a to locate some neighborhood places.

☐ b that being polite is important.

☐ c to talk about my favorite places in my neighborhood.

1 Read and write the words.

exhibit   doctor   ~~conductor~~   security guard   alarm   firefighter

a A __conductor__ works on a train.

b A _____ can put out fires.

c An _____ goes off when there's fire.

d A _____ helps sick people.

e There's an _____ in the museum.

f A _____ takes care of a place.

2 Look and unscramble the words.

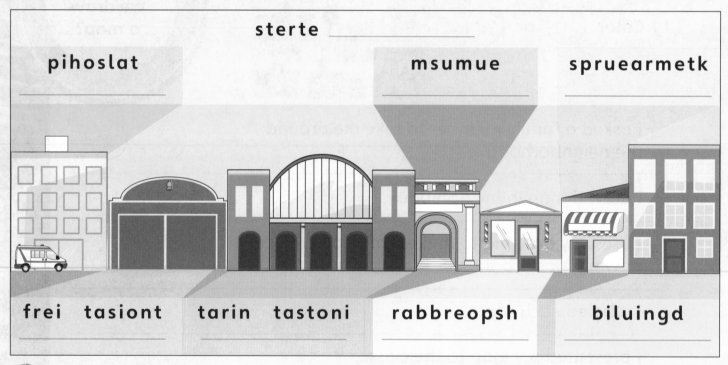

sterte _____

pihoslat _____

msumue _____

spruearmetk _____

frei tasiont _____

tarin tastoni _____

rabbreopsh _____

biluingd _____

3 Write the words.

greet   ~~city~~   break   wax   flashlight

WAX MUSEUM

There's a museum in the 1__city__.
There are many 2_____ statues in it.
One statue looks like a superhero. When I visit the museum, I always 3_____ him, but he never greets me back. Another wax statue has a bright 4_____. This statue looks like a security guard, but he never takes a 5_____!

18

4) Look and answer the questions.

Zac	Saturday	afternoon	
Alicia	Monday	morning $12 \div 3 =$	

a When does Zac play soccer? He plays soccer __on Saturday__ .

b When does he read? He reads _____ .

c What time does he eat lunch? He eats lunch _____ .

d When does Alicia play the piano? She plays the piano _____ .

e When does she have math? She has math _____ .

f What time does she ride her bike? She rides her bike _____ .

5) Look and match.

1 The train station is

2 The park is

3 The fire station is

4 The trees are

a in front of the library.

b behind the museum.

c between the museum and the library.

d in front of the museum.

train station

library

museum

fire station

park

6) Label the pictures.

butterfly   birdhouse   fire station   ~~bus stop~~   forty-five

a bus stop

b _____

c _____

d _____

e _____

SPEAKING MISSION

1 **Look and mark ✓ the places in your neighborhood.**

2 **Look at the photos in Activity I and number the places.**

- [5] sports center
- [ ] candy store
- [ ] bank
- [ ] zoo
- [ ] grocery store
- [ ] movie theater

3 **Number the dialogue lines in order.**
- [ ] Thank you!
- [ ] First, walk for two blocks.
- [1] Excuse me. How can I get to the movie theater?
- [ ] Then, turn right.
- [6] You're welcome!
- [ ] The movie theater is in front of the zoo.

What can you remember about ... Unit 1?

① **Circle the correct word.**

There are exhibits in a **hospital / museum**.

② **Circle the adjectives.**

big   conductor   beautiful
small   firefighter

③ **What is this? Circle the correct word.**

a flashlight
an alarm
a street

④ **Unscramble the question.**

Where's / bus stop / the / ?

_____

It's between the park and the museum.

⑤ **Where do Carlos and his mom get some ice cream?**

at the _____

⑥ **Circle the two words that have the same sound as *rain*.**

may   help   take

⑦ **Look and complete this sentence.**

He has a piano lesson

_____ .

⑧ **Unscramble and write the words.**

fshlaghtli _____

aalrm _____

⑨ **Circle the correct word.**

They play **in / on** Fridays.

_____

⑩ **Read and match.**

at   Monday
on   November
in   three o'clock

Check your answers in the Student's Book. How did you do?

7–10 ☐ Great!   4–6 ☐ Good!   0–3 ☐ Try harder!

❓ 😄 What is in my neighborhood? Write your answers to the Big Question.

_____

_____

2 Why are celebrations important?

1 ▶ 2.1 **Watch the video. Complete the graphic organizer.**

candy   candles   ~~celebrate~~   present   balloons

You put _____ on a birthday cake.

Your friends can give you _____ a birthday _____.

How do you _celebrate_ your birthday?

There is _____ inside a piñata.

You can decorate with _____ and confetti.

2 Key Words 1 **Read the sentences and circle the correct words.**

a

People **celebrate** / **give** New Year around the world.

b

There is sometimes a big **piñata** / **balloon** with the words *Happy New Year!*

c

In some countries people give each other a **present** / **cake**.

Ready to Read: Nonfiction

1 Key Words 2 **Circle the words in the word search. Then, label the pictures.**

~~birthday~~   give   party   invite   light   wish   open

a

birthday

b

l	i	g	h	t	u	o	p	e	n
j	k	i	o	w	k	l	a	o	e
a	s	d	g	i	v	e	r	e	r
c	v	r	t	s	u	i	t	p	l
b	i	r	t	h	d	a	y	u	o
w	e	r	t	y	b	n	a	a	q
k	i	n	v	i	t	e	w	i	d

c

d

e

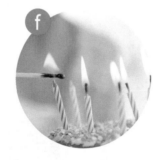

f

g

2 **Complete the sentences with words from Activity I.**

a I always __invite__ my friends to my birthday _____.

b They _____ me many presents.

c Mom and Dad _____ the candles on my birthday cake.

d Then, I make a _____ and blow out the candles.

e My friends and I play games, and I _____ their presents. They're nice!

Reading Strategy: Comparing and Contrasting

We compare things when we tell how they are similar.
We contrast things when we tell how they are different.

1. **Read the texts and circle the answers.**

Vick has four small balloons. His balloons are red, green, yellow, and blue.

Kira has five small balloons. Her balloons are yellow, red, pink, blue, and green.

Who has ...

a	some small balloons?	Vick	Kira	Both
b	a red balloon?	Vick	Kira	Both
c	four balloons?	Vick	Kira	Both
d	a pink balloon?	Vick	Kira	Both
e	a blue balloon?	Vick	Kira	Both

2. **Read the text.**

My Brother and I

Hello! My name is Simon and this is my brother, Ryan. We wear similar clothes. Our shirts are the same, but our pants are different. Ryan is wearing long pants, but my pants are short. We like the same colors. Our favorite color is blue.

Today is my birthday. I'm eight years old, and Ryan is six. His birthday is in April. We usually have a birthday party, and we always have a big birthday cake. Ryan likes chocolate, but I prefer vanilla. My mom bakes delicious cakes for us. We put some candles on them. Look! Mom is lighting the candle on my birthday cake!

Ryan is excited about my birthday party. He's waiting for our friends to come. We want to play with them. I want to ride a bike, and Ryan wants to play soccer. We can do both things!

24

③ **Circle the words.**

a Ryan is Simon's (brother)/ friend.

b Simon is **six** / **eight** years old.

c Ryan is wearing **long** / **short** pants.

d Their favorite color is **blue** / **white**.

e Ryan likes **vanilla** / **chocolate** cake.

f They want to play **the same** / **different** games.

④ **Read again and write *S* for same or *D* for different.**

	👕	👖	💧	68	🎂	🚴
Simon and Ryan	S	___	___	___	___	___

⑤ **Read and complete the graphic organizer.**

> seven ~~tiger~~ cookies cupcakes ladybug

Nina and Alexa are seven years old. Their birthday party is on Saturday. They want to wear costumes to their party. Nina wants to dress like a tiger, and Alexa wants to dress like a ladybug. Nina wants cupcakes, but Alexa wants cookies.

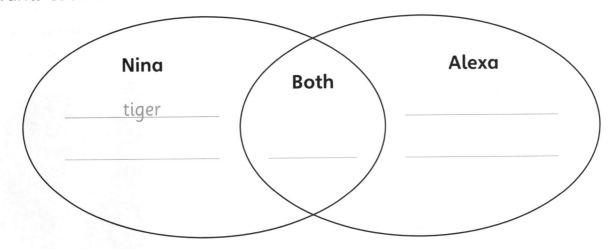

Nina

tiger

_____

Both

_____

Alexa

_____

_____

Grammar in Context

Adverbs of Frequency: *always, usually, sometimes, never*

I **always** celebrate my birthday. My friends **sometimes** eat candy.
We **usually** play at the park. We **never** watch TV.

always ✓✓✓✓✓, usually ✓✓✓, sometimes ✓✓, never ✗

1 **Read and color the boxes.**

a In China, people always celebrate their Spring Festival, or New Year, between January and February.
     ✓✓✓   ✓✓✓✓✓

b Families usually have dinner together.
     ✓✓✓   ✓✓

c They sometimes give each other money in red envelopes as a present.
     ✗   ✓✓

d Chinese people never stop celebrating New Year.
     ✓✓✓   ✗

e They always eat delicious food and make a wish for good luck.
     ✓✓✓✓✓   ✓✓✓

2 **Look and circle the correct words.**

a My friend Myriam **usually** / **sometimes** sings. ✓✓

b Clara and Hugo **sometimes** / **usually** read a poem. ✓✓✓

c Our parents **always** / **sometimes** go to the festival. ✓✓✓✓✓

d My classmates **never** / **usually** play the piano. ✗

e They **sometimes** / **always** play the guitar. ✓✓

At school, we have a special festival every year.

26

3 Unscramble the sentences. Then, number the pictures.

1 We / in the United States / celebrate / Independence Day / always

We always celebrate Independence Day in the United States.

2 usually / have / We / fireworks

_____

3 Families / together / dinner / always / have

_____

4 usually / wear / hats / red, white, and blue / We

_____

5 bake / cupcakes / sometimes / People

_____

 1

4 Look and write sentences.

a
He / ✓✓✓ / wear / costume

He usually wears a costume.

b
They / ✗ / look sad

_____ .

c
They / ✓✓ / put on
paper masks

_____ .

d
He / ✓✓✓✓✓ / make
a wish

_____ .

My Life

Write about yourself.

I always _____ .

I sometimes _____ .

1 **Read the riddles and circle the words with the long *i* sound as in *light*. Then, number the pictures.**

a bike

a slide

1

a kite

1
It's not heavy, it's (light),
and it can be white.
And in the blue sky,
it can fly.

2
Up you can climb
from just one side
then down take a ride
to have a good time!

3
On it you can ride
with your friend Mike
or your neighbor Spike
if that's what you like.

2 **Cross out the words in each line with a different vowel sound.**

a ~~say~~   fly   side   time

b bike   Mike   take   like

c ride   wake   hike   kite

3 **Match the words that rhyme.**

a Spike   sky

b light   bike

c fly   ride

d slide   kite

1 **Complete the expressions.**

awesome   job   ~~Good~~

a Look at my card!   _____Good_____ work!

b This is my photo.   It's _____!

c I wrote this riddle.   Great _____!

Improve Your Writing: Synonyms

Synonyms are words with similar meanings:
unhappy – sad, loud – noisy, hard – difficult, angry – mad.

1 **Match the synonyms.**

big   little

small   quiet

silent   quick

fast   pretty

beautiful   large

2 **Complete the invitation. Then, circle the synonym for *pretty*.**

Saturday, August 10   ~~Party~~   11 a.m.   backyard

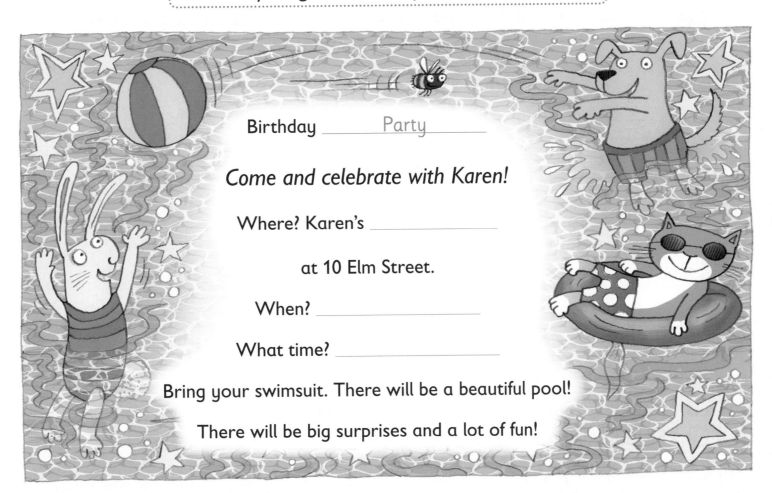

Birthday _____Party_____

Come and celebrate with Karen!

Where? Karen's _____

at 10 Elm Street.

When? _____

What time? _____

Bring your swimsuit. There will be a beautiful pool!

There will be big surprises and a lot of fun!

Writing

1 READ Read the invitation on page 29 and answer the questions.

a Whose party is it? It's _____ party.

b Where is it? It's at _____ .

c When is it? It's on _____ .

d What time is the party? It's at _____ .

e What do you bring to the party? You bring your _____ .

2 PLAN Complete the chart about your birthday party.

Where?	When?	What Time?	What to Bring?	What Will Be There?

3 WRITE Write your birthday party invitation. Then, decorate and color it.

Come to my birthday party!

_____

_____

_____

_____

_____

4 EDIT Check ✓.

WRITING CHECKLIST

☐ I included the place/address, date, and time.

☐ I included *What to bring*.

☐ I used synonyms.

30

| Unit 2B | **Ready to Read:** Fiction |

1 Key Words 4 **Circle the letters to form words. Then, label the pictures.**

a

ⓓa ⓔⓣⓔ ⓢ ⓒⓣu o ⓘ b ⓥⓔ

detective

b

tghiwef

_____

c

buosraed

_____

d

skcasretd

_____

e

tournuofgn

_____

f

tusrmnuoff

_____

2 **Complete the sentences. Use words from Activity I.**

a In the school play, I am a _____detective_____ .

b Bill is a _____ .

c Our parents come to see the play. They are not _____ because it's fun!

d When the play ends, we _____ the lights. It's dark.

e We hear a sound. Now we are _____!

f Raul and Salim _____ the lights. There's a vase on the floor!

31

Reading Strategy: Cause and Effect

An effect is what happens. A cause is why something happens.

(1) **Read the first sentence. Then, circle two possible effects.**

Today is Mindy's costume party.

a Mindy dresses up like a princess.
c Ava puts on a clown's costume.

b Sally goes to the park.

(2) **Read the story.**

A Costume Party

Today is Mindy's birthday. Mindy invites her friends to her costume party. Mindy wants to be a princess. She puts on a long, purple dress and a pink hat. She puts on a big bright ring, too. Mindy's friend, Ava, dresses up as a clown. She's wearing big black shoes and colorful pants. Her friend, Adam, is a detective.

Mindy and her friends play games. They are never bored. Then, Mindy's mother puts a chocolate cake on the table and turns off the lights. They all sing *Happy Birthday*! Mindy takes off her ring and puts it on the cake. She makes a wish and blows out the candles! The room is dark.

Mindy's mother turns on the lights. Mindy's ring is not on the cake! Adam looks for the ring on the table. It's not there! Adam looks for the ring in the candy bowls. It's not there!

Then, he looks for the ring under the table. There's a little bright thing that walks. He looks at it. It's an ant on the floor! It's carrying Mindy's ring!

③ **Circle the correct statements.**

a Mindy invites her friends to the party.

Mindy invites her grandparents to the party.

b Mindy is wearing a purple hat.

Mindy is wearing a purple dress.

c Ava's pants are black.

Ava's pants are colorful.

d Mindy turns off the lights.

Mindy's mother turns off the lights.

e The ring is under the table.

The ring is on the table.

④ **Match the causes with the effects.**

Cause	Effect
1 Today is Mindy's birthday.	a They aren't bored.
2 Mindy's friends play games.	b Adam looks for the ring.
3 The ring is not on the cake.	c She invites her friends.

⑤ **Circle the cause and underline the effect.**

a Mindy wants a costume party. All her friends wear costumes.

b Mindy wants to be a princess. She puts on a long, purple dress and a pink hat.

c Mindy's mom makes a chocolate birthday cake. Mindy loves chocolate.

d Mindy's mother turns off the lights. It's dark.

Subject and Object Pronouns

> Zac **is in the park with** his friends. = He **is in the park with** them.
> Laura and Wendy **give** Sue **a present.** = They **give** her **a present.**
> Pat and I **see the cat.** = We **see** it.

(1) Match the subject with the object pronouns.

Subject Pronouns   I   you   he   she   it   we   they

Object Pronouns   him   me   them   you   us   it   her

(2) Circle the pronouns.

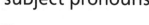 = subject pronouns   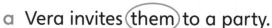 = object pronouns

a Vera invites (them) to a party.

b Grandpa and Grandma bring a large present for her.

c Vera puts it on a table.

d Then, she plays with Sarah.

e Vera says, "We are good friends!"

f Sarah says, "Please give us some cake!"

(3) Rewrite the sentences. Replace the underlined words with pronouns.

a Hilda and I are good friends.

   We are good friends.

b I can give Hilda a storybook on her birthday.

   _____

c Will she like the storybook?

   _____

d Grandma reads Hilda and me stories.

4 Complete the sentences.

a My friends are at the party. __They__ are wearing party hats.

b Gina is hitting the piñata. _____ is colorful.

c Those are my presents. We put _____ on the table.

d Mom made my cake. I said *Thank you* to _____ .

e Thelma is my cousin. _____ is at my party, too.

5 Look and complete the dialogues.

What do your parents give ___you___ on your birthday?

They give _____ some nice presents.

Are Tim and Sue at your party?

Yes, _____ are.

My Life

Circle the correct pronouns. Write about a family celebration.

a My family and **I / me** celebrate _____ .

b **They / We** eat _____ to celebrate _____ .

c _____

1 **Look and circle the pictures.**

= giving

= receiving

a — Thank you!

b — This is for you, Mom!

c — I like it!

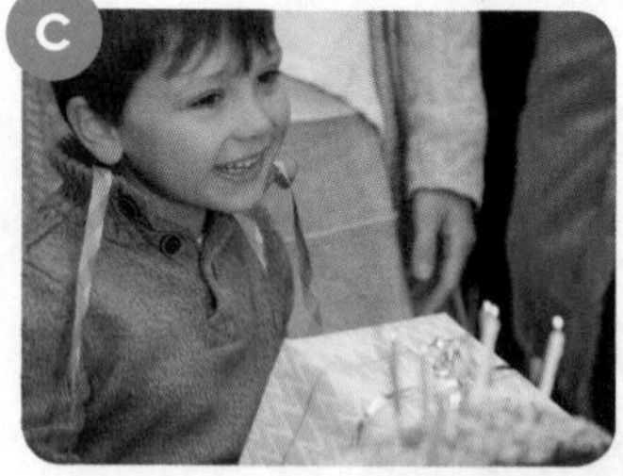

d — I'm baking cookies for you!

e — Thanks!

2 **Color the expressions that you use for giving.**

This is for you!   Thanks!

Thank you!   I'm giving you a card!

These flowers are for you, Mom!   They're beautiful!

3 **Draw yourself giving something to someone in your family.**

Check Your Oracy!

Read and circle *Yes* or *No*.

1 I presented my card.   **Yes / No**

2 I gave positive feedback.   **Yes / No**

3 I responded to positive feedback.   **Yes / No**

The Big Challenge

 How can we make a gift for Mom?

(1) **Color** **or** .

I folded a sheet of colored cardboard to make a card.		
I drew, cut out, and glued a flower onto the card.		
I glued a picture of myself in the center of the flower.		
I wrote *I love you!* inside the card.		
I signed my card and displayed it on my desk.		
I looked at my classmates' cards and complimented them.		

The Big Question and (**Me**)

Think and mark ✓. **In Unit 2, I learned …**

☐ a to talk about parties.

☐ b that giving is important.

☐ c to say how we celebrate things.

1 **Complete the words.**

a
c <u>a</u> <u>k</u> e

b
c _ _ d l _

c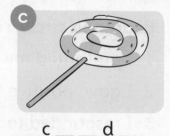
c _ _ d _

d
p _ e _ e _ t

e
b _ l l _ _ n

f
c _ l e _ _ a t _

2 **Look and complete the sentences. Then, number the pictures.**

invite ~~party~~ cover open coin light

1 The girls are at the _____ party _____ .

2 He wants to _____ his presents.

3 Mom can _____ the candles on the cake.

4 He wants to _____ his friend to a party.

5 She always makes a wish as she flips a _____ .

6 I _____ my eyes before I hit the piñata.

a
b
c  1
d
e
f

3 **Look and circle the words.**

a
detective / (thief)

b
scared / bored

c
turn on / turn off

d
detective / thief

e
scared / bored

4 **Look and complete the sentences.**

a Clara ___always___ has fun with her friends.

b She _____ rides her bike.

c She _____ reads stories.

d She _____ plays video games.

5 **Circle the pronouns in the sentences and complete the chart.**

a Grandma tells my brother and (me) a story.

b (We) like it.

c It's about a celebration.

d She gives us some pictures.

e They show her in a costume.

f Do you want to learn about this celebration?

Subject Pronouns			Object Pronouns		
I _____ she _____ _we_ _____			_me_ you him _____ _____ them		

6 **Match the synonyms.**

pretty   silent   fast   big   little

quick   large   small   beautiful   quiet

SPEAKING MISSION

1 Look and mark ✓ what you like to eat at a celebration. Then, label the pictures.

> popcorn   chocolates   jello   ~~cupcakes~~   potato chips   ice cream

1

☐

cupcakes

2

☐

_____

3

☐

_____

4

☐

_____

5

☐

_____

6

☐

_____

2 Number the dialogue lines in order.

☐ Thank you!

☐ Hi! How can I help you?

☐ Here you are!

1 Hello!

☐ How much is it?

☐ I want some popcorn, please.

☐ Two dollars, please.

☐ Good-bye!

What can you remember about ... Unit 2?

1 **Write these words in alphabetical order.**

candy birthday cake balloon

_____

_____

_____

_____

2 **Circle the synonyms.**

fast silent quick

3 **What is this?**

a candle a ring a coin

4 **Circle the subject pronoun.**

Jenny and I will visit our aunt.

5 **Where is Mrs. Smith's diamond necklace?**

In Mia's _____'s hair.

6 **Which two words have the same sound as _slide_?**

hide make kite

7 **Look and complete these words.**

ice _____

cup _____

8 **Unscramble and write the words.**

rebod _____

csreda _____

9 **Circle the correct adverb of frequency.**

They **always / sometimes** play ball. ✓✓

10 **Circle the object pronoun.**

I see them at the park.

Check your answers in the Student's Book. How did you do?

7–10 ☐ Great!   4–6 ☐ Good!   0–3 ☐ Try harder!

? 😀 Why are celebrations important?

To have fun with _____ and _____ .

3 Why is food important?

1 ▶ 3.1 **Watch the video. Complete the graphic organizer.**

watermelon   carrots   ice cream   chicken   ~~salad~~   sandwich

Today's Menu

___Salad___
vegetable
fruit

Fruit
apples
_____

Good and Crunchy!
fried _____

_____

Sweet Protein!
peanut butter and jelly _____
_____ (with the best milk)

2 Key Words 1 **Circle the words and number the pictures.**

1 (Ice cream) / **Watermelon**
has milk.

2 You can have a jelly or a
chicken **cookie / sandwich**.

3 **Carrots / Cupcakes** have lot
of vitamins.

4 Be careful with the seeds in
chicken / watermelon.

5 Do you like vegetable **salad /
cookies**?

6 Fried **milk / chicken** is crunchy.

a   b   c 1

d   e   f

1 Key Words 2 Decode the words.

a = ●   e = ●   i = ●   o = ●   u = ●

1 b ● n ● n ●   _banana_

2 r ● c ●   _____

3 y ● g ● r t   _____

4 s ● g ● r   _____

5 p ● s t ●   _____

6 t ● m ● t ●   _____

7 m ● l k   _____

2 Complete the sentences. Use words from Activity I. Number the pictures.

a

b   1

c

d

e

f

g

1 There is a ___banana___ on that plate.

2 There's only one _____. It's red.

3 Ice cream and _____ have milk.

4 There are lots of _____ cubes on the table.

5 There's some _____ in the glass.

6 The _____ is in that brown bowl.

7 There is some cheese on the _____.

1 **Match the underlined parts of the text with the questions.**

Kiwifruit or <u>kiwi</u> is a soft fruit that comes from <u>China.</u> Kiwifruit is <u>brown on the outside and green on the inside</u>. A kiwi can have <u>1,500</u> small seeds!

a Where is kiwifruit from?

b What is a short name for kiwifruit?

c How many seeds can a kiwi have?

d What color is kiwi?

2 **Read the text.**

EAT *Healthy,*
STAY *Strong*

Healthy food is good for you. When we eat healthy food we stay strong.

Green and orange vegetables are good for your body. They have lots of vitamins and minerals that you need to be healthy. Carrots are good for your eyes, too. Broccoli makes you strong. Look! There are many vegetables in this salad.

Some salads are made with fruit. Fruit has vitamins that help you stay healthy. Vitamins help you get better when you are sick, too. This fruit salad is very colorful!

Pasta and rice give you energy. When you are going to run and play a lot, eat pasta and rice! You can eat them with vegetables, chicken, or fish. This is a plate of fried rice with vegetables. It looks delicious!

Protein is in foods like chicken, fish, and milk. There is protein in some seeds and nuts, too. Protein makes your body strong and healthy.

Milk is yummy and has a lot of protein. There is milk in cheese, yogurt and ice cream, too. Mix some yogurt with your favorite fruit like this!

44

③ **Mark ✓ the words.**

a Vitamins and minerals: ☑ fruit ☐ chicken ☐ vegetables

b Protein: ☐ milk ☐ pasta ☐ fish

c Energy: ☐ broccoli ☐ rice ☐ pasta

④ **Look and label each picture.**

V = vitamins P = protein E = energy

a b c d e

P ☐ ☐ ☐ ☐

⑤ **Read and circle the answers to these questions.**

a Where do watermelons come from?

b Where do farmers grow square watermelons?

c What color are watermelons on the outside?

d Do all watermelons have seeds?

e How much of a watermelon is water?

Watermelons

Watermelons come from Africa. Most watermelons are round, but in Japan, farmers grow square watermelons. They look like big cubes. Watermelons are green on the outside and red on the inside. There are a lot of seeds in most of them, but in some countries, farmers grow them without any seeds. Watermelons are good when the weather is hot. A watermelon is 92% water!

Quantifiers: *a lot of, some, any*

There is **a lot of milk** in the fridge.
There are **a lot of carrots** in the basket.
We need **some fruit** for the cake.
Eat **some vegetables** every day.
I **don't have any rice**.
She **isn't eating any seeds**.

What's in the fridge?

(1) **Look and mark ✓.**

a ☑ There are a lot of carrots.   ☐ There aren't any carrots.

b ☐ We have some chicken.   ☐ We don't have any chicken.

c ☐ There are only three bananas.   ☐ There are a lot of bananas.

d ☐ I see a lot of yogurt.   ☐ I don't see any yogurt.

e ☐ There is some milk.   ☐ There isn't any milk.

(2) **Look and circle the words.**

a There are **(a lot of)** / **any** vegetables and fruits.

b We don't have **any** / **some** broccoli.

c There are **any** / **some** carrots and tomatoes.

d There are seven bananas. There are **any** / **a lot of** them.

e There isn't **any** / **some** watermelon.

f I can see **some** / **any** apples, too.

3 Complete the sentences.

> some   a lot of   any

 **a**

Let's have a picnic! There's <u>a lot of</u> cheese. Let's make cheese sandwiches.

b

Let's make _____ salad, too.

c

There aren't _____ tomatoes!

d

We have 30 plates. There are _____ plates!

e

Can you bring _____ watermelon?

f

There isn't _____ fruit.

4 Look and write sentences.

a
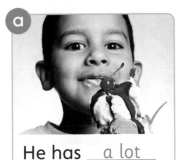
He has __a lot__
__of ice cream__ .

b

I don't want ____
_____ .

c

There is _____
_____ .

d
There aren't ____
_____ .

My Life

Write about your lunchbox.

There **is / are** some _____ .

There **is / are** a lot of _____ .

There **isn't / aren't** any _____ .

Phonics

(1) **Circle the words that sound like** *o* **in** *Rose*. **Then, number the pictures.**

1 Do you want a (scone) or an ice cream cone?

2 Does he have a boat or a coat?

3 Where do you go in that dress with a bow?

4 Can you see that old, bold tree?

5 Do you like yogurt or yolks?

(2) **Cross out the words in each line with a different vowel sound.**

a Rose boat yolk ~~blond~~   b bow plate cold home

c goat lot old cone   d coat long scone go

(3) **Circle the words to complete the rhymes.**

a There was a goat close to the **lot /** (**boat**.)

b I am putting my scone inside that **cone / bowl**.

c Will you see Rose where she always **stops / goes**?

Oracy

(1) **Circle the correct expressions**

a I think tomato soup is delicious.   **I agree. / I disagree.** It's really good!

b Chocolate ice cream is the best.   **I agree. / I disagree.** I like vanilla ice cream.

c I think watermelon is really good.   **I agree. / I disagree.** It's my favorite!

Improve Your Writing: Antonyms

Antonyms are words with opposite meanings.
happy – sad, same – different, tall – short, old – new, sweet – sour

1 **Color the antonyms.**

a big   small   fast   d happy   sad   good

b fast   small   slow   e good   quiet   bad

c hot   cold   bad   f old   large   little

2 **Circle the correct antonym.**

Fruit Salad

INGREDIENTS

3 different fruits

¼ cup of honey

½ cup of small nuts

½ cup of raisins

First, ask an adult to chop the **same / different** fruits into pieces.

Next, put the fruit in a **large / little** bowl.

Then, add the **sweet / sour** honey, **big / small** nuts, and **wet / dry** raisins.

Finally, mix the ingredients with a **clean / dirty** spoon and enjoy your salad!

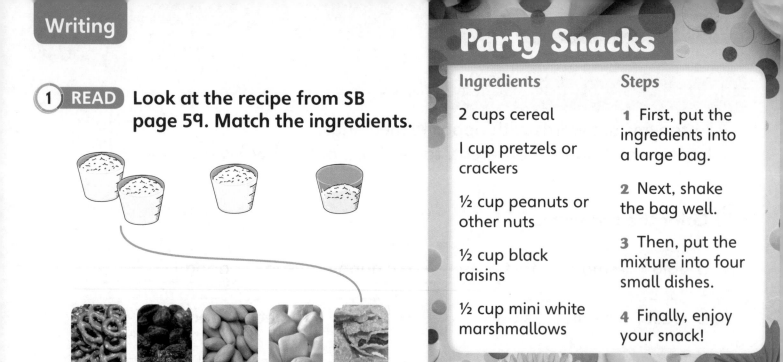

1 READ Look at the recipe from SB page 59. Match the ingredients.

Party Snacks

Ingredients	Steps
2 cups cereal	**1** First, put the ingredients into a large bag.
I cup pretzels or crackers	**2** Next, shake the bag well.
½ cup peanuts or other nuts	**3** Then, put the mixture into four small dishes.
½ cup black raisins	**4** Finally, enjoy your snack!
½ cup mini white marshmallows	

2 Circle the sequence words in the recipe.

3 PLAN WRITE Complete the chart about your recipe. Then, write the steps.

Name: _____

Ingredients: Steps:
_____   First, _____
_____   _____
_____   _____
_____   _____
_____   _____
_____   _____
_____   _____

4 EDIT Check ✓.

WRITING CHECKLIST

☐ I listed the ingredients and steps.   ☐ I included antonyms.

☐ I used *First*, *Next*, *Then*, and *Finally*.

(1) Key Words 4 **Unscramble the words and label the pictures.**

a

ouflr
flour

b

whtea
_____

c

eadbr
_____

d

enov
_____

e

xim
_____

f

ghoud
_____

(2) **Complete the sentences. Use words from Activity I.**

Let's make some 1 _bread_ . We need some water and wheat 2_____ . Put the ingredients in a bowl and 3_____ them. Use your hands to knead the 4_____ . Then, let it rest for a few hours. Finally, cook the dough in the 5_____ . When the bread is ready, eat it with some jelly!

Reading Strategy: Identifying Characters

The characters are the people, animals, and sometimes the objects in a story.

(1) **Circle the characters from the story in Activity 2.**

(2) **Read the story.**

Little Red Hen
Russian Folk Tale

Little Red Hen lives on a farm with her chicks. One day she finds some seeds. She has an idea.

I will plant these seeds!

Little Red Hen asks her friends Cat, Duck, and Rat for help.

Who will help me plant the seeds?

Not I!

Then I will.

When the seeds grow, Little Red Hen wants to cut the wheat.

Who will help me cut the wheat?

Not I!

Then I will.

Little Red Hen wants to make the flour.

Who will help me make the flour?

Not I!

Then I will.

Now it is time to make the bread.

Who will help me make the bread?

Not I!

Then I will.

Then, Little Red Hen makes the dough and bakes the bread.

Who will eat this bread?

I will!

No, you won't. We will!

Little Red Hen and her chicks eat up all the bread.

3 **Number Little Red Hen's words in order.**

☐ "Who will help me make the flour?"

[1] "Who will help me plant the seeds?"

☐ "Who will eat this bread?"

☐ "Who will help me cut the wheat?"

☐ "Who will help me make the bread?"

4 **Match the descriptions with the characters.**

a   This character is white. He doesn't help make the bread.

b   This character is red. She likes working.

c   This character is gray. She has a long tail.

d   This character is brown. He doesn't like working.

○ Rat

○ Little Red Hen

○ Cat

○ Duck

5 **Look at the book covers and titles. Then, number the characters.**

[2] Mama Bear

☐ Goldilocks

☐ Jack

☐ Jack's mother

☐ Ugly Duckling

☐ Papa Bear

How much ... ? How many ... ?

How much **flour** is **there?**   How many **eggs** are **there?**

1 Circle *much* or *many*. Then, number the answers.

 1 How **many** / **much** raisins are there?

 2 How **many** / **much** sugar is there?

 3 How **many** / **much** bananas are there?

 4 How **many** / **much** nuts are there?

☐ There are four.

☐ There is one cup.

☐ There are two.

1 There are five.

2 Complete and answer the questions.

How much   How many

a How much cake is there? There are ___two___ pieces of cake.

b _____ ice cream cones are there? There are _____ ice cream cones.

c _____ chocolate ice cream is there? There is _____ cone.

d _____ ice cream cups are there? There are _____ cups.

e _____ green cupcakes are there? There is _____ green cupcake.

f _____ milk is there? There is _____ glass of milk.

Special Treats
and More!

3 Circle *is* or *are*. Then, complete the answers.

a How much yogurt **is** / **are** there?

There ____are____ two cups of yogurt.

b How many strawberries **is** / **are** there?

There _____ ten strawberries.

c How much honey **is** / **are** there?

There _____ one jar.

d How many cups **is** / **are** there?

There _____ three cups.

Let's make breakfast!

4 Look and write questions with *how much* and *how many*.

a

apples

How many apples are there?

b

bread

c

orange juice

d

sandwiches

My Life

Answer the questions about yourself.

a How much milk do you drink every day? _____

b How many different vegetables do you like? _____

1 **Look and match.**

☐ Thanks, Mom! I love milk.

☐ Dad's orange juice is the best!

☐ Thanks a lot for setting the table, Daniel!

[a] Thanks for helping me make these cookies.

2 **Color the expressions that you use to show gratitude.**

Your cookies are the best, Grandma!　　Thank you!　　Thanks a lot!

I don't want this food!　　I love your salad!　　Your cookies are bad!

3 **Draw yourself showing your gratitude to someone in your family.**

Check Your Oracy!

Read and circle *Yes* or *No*.

1 I gave my opinion.   **Yes / No**

2 I listened to my partner's opinion.   **Yes / No**

3 I respected my partner's opinion.   **Yes / No**

How can we eat a healthy lunch?

The Big Challenge

(1) Color  or  .

I looked at the Healthy Eating Guide on page 53.	☺ ☹
I thought of healthy options for my lunch.	☺ ☹
I chose foods from different sections of the guide.	☺ ☹
I made a drawing of my healthy lunch.	☺ ☹
I prepared my healthy lunch and brought it to school.	☺ ☹
I presented my lunch to the class.	☺ ☹

The Big Question and **Me**

Think and mark ✓. In Unit 3, I learned …

☐ a to talk about healthy food.

☐ b that gratitude is important.

☐ c why we need to eat different foods to be healthy.

1 **Guess the riddles and write the words.**

> salad   watermelon   ~~tomato~~   banana   carrot

a Round and red it is, and there are many vitamins in it.   ___tomato___

b It's green outside and red inside, and it's 92% water.   _____

c To be healthy, you can eat this long, orange, and crunchy vegetable.   _____

d It's colorful and healthy. There are many foods in it.   _____

e It's a long, soft, yellow fruit, and it's good for breakfast.   _____

2 **Look and complete the words.**

a

There's c _h_ ic _k_ en, r____e, and vegetables.

b

There's a s__n___i__h and some p____t__.

c

How much __ce c__e__m is there?

d

Is that s__g__r or flour?

e

Does yo____r__have m____k in it?

3 **Look and circle the words.**

a
There are **a lot of** / **any** apples.

b
There isn't **a lot of** / **any** bread.

c
There are **any** / **some** nuts.

d
There is **some** / **any** wheat.

4 **Look and complete the sentences.**

> many   much

a How ___much___ cake is there?
There is **some** / **any** cake.

b How _____ bananas are there?
There are **a lot of** / **any** bananas.

c How _____ watermelon is there?
There is **any** / **some** watermelon.

d How _____ tomatoes are there?
There aren't **a lot of** / **any** tomatoes.

5 **Color the antonyms in matching colors.**

large

good

hot

sad

bad

cold

happy

small

(1) Look and circle the words.

a · **eggs** / yogurt

b · chicken / fish

c · broccoli / peas

d · melon / tomatoes

e · apple juice / orange juice

f · rice / pasta

(2) Write the words in each section.

eggs   milk
~~melon~~   bread
fish   rice   peas

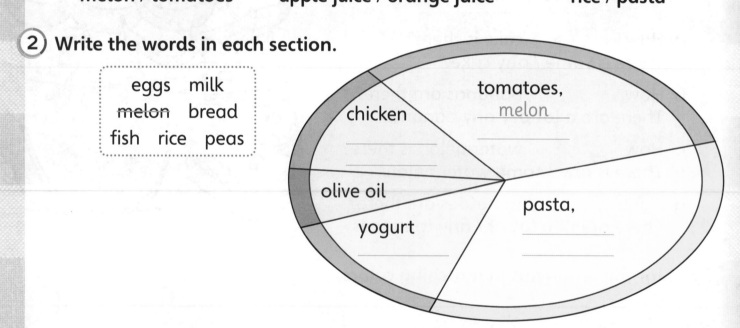

chicken

tomatoes, _melon_

olive oil

yogurt

pasta,

(3) Number the dialogue lines in order.

[ ] I agree. There's protein in chicken, and pasta gives you energy.

[1] Let's have some chicken and pasta for lunch.

[ ] That's important. Vegetables have vitamins.

[ ] I think we can make a vegetable salad, too.

[ ] That's awesome! I like vanilla!

[ ] Finally, let's buy some ice cream!

What can you remember about ... Unit 3?

① Complete these words with the same two letters.

w h _ _ t   b r _ _ d
p l _ t _   w _ t _ r m _ l o n

② Circle the antonyms.

hot   large   cold

③ What are these?

glasses   cups

plates

④ Circle the correct words.

How **many** / **much** milk is there?

There isn't **some** / **any** milk.

There is **some** / **any** apple juice.

⑤ Which character eats the little bread bun?

the bear   the fox   the rabbit

⑥ Which two words have the same sound as co**at.**

bow   blond   yolk

⑦ Look and write the word.

_____

⑧ Look and write *a lot of* or *some*.

There is _____ bread.

There are _____ cookies.

⑨ Circle three words that you use in a recipe.

always   first   then

usually   finally

⑩ Unscramble the question.

much / How / is / ice cream / there / ?

_____

Check your answers in the Student's Book. How did you do?
7–10 ☐ Great!   4–6 ☐ Good!   0–3 ☐ Try harder!

? 😀 Why is food important?

Food makes your body strong and _____ .

4 How does our planet change?

1 ▶ 4.1 **Watch the video. Complete the graphic organizer.**

~~rain~~   mountain   volcano   beach   river   lake

water 🌀   rock ●

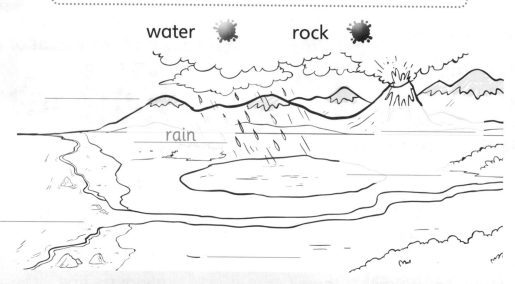

rain

2 **Key Words 1** **Complete the sentences with words from Activity I. Then, number the pictures.**

a

1 ___Rain___ and snow fall to the ground and into oceans, rivers, and lakes.

2 A _____ carries water to the ocean.

3 Many fish and other animals live in a _____ .

4 The waves of the ocean crash against rocks and make a _____ .

5 There's hot lava in an active _____ .

6 Volcanoes sometimes form a _____ .

b

c 1

d
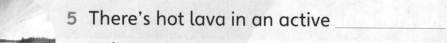

e

f

SB pages 72–73

1 Key Words 2 **Circle the words and match them with the pictures.**

a   b   c   d

shake cornfield scientist hill fire grow ash

e   f   g

2 Complete the sentences with words from Activity I.

a

This is a ___cornfield___ . First, farmers plant seeds in the ground. These seeds _____ into corn.

b

Rocks under the ground _____ . The volcano is now active. _____ and fire come out of it.

c

A _____ is on the farm. He's looking at some plants from that _____ .

Reading Strategy: Sequencing

Sequence is the order of events.

1 **Look and number the pictures.**

a
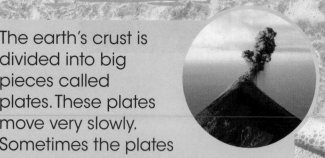

b
1

c

d

2 **Read the text.**

Volcanoes and Beaches

The earth's crust is divided into big pieces called plates. These plates move very slowly. Sometimes the plates push against each other, and they make a volcano!

Volcanoes erupt. That means that lava, ash, and gases come out of the volcano. It's very, very hot!

There are active and dormant volcanoes. Active volcanoes erupt. Dormant volcanoes do not erupt, but they can become active in the future.

When you go to the beach, you can see sand. Sand can be many different colors. You can see beaches with white sand, brown sand, black sand, and even pink sand!

But what is sand? And where does it come from? Sand is made of tiny pieces of rocks and shells. The ocean makes sand! First, the ocean waves hit rocks along the shore. Next, the big rocks break down into small rocks. Then, the small rocks break down again into tiny rocks. Finally, the rocks are so tiny that they are not rocks. They are sand!

64

3 **Read and circle the correct words.**

a Sometimes the earth's plates move and make mountains and **oceans / volcanoes**.

b Gases and lava from a volcano are very **cold / hot**.

c A volcano which is **dormant / active** is erupting.

d The **ocean waves / rain** make sand.

e Sand can be different colors, such as white, pink, and **purple / black**.

f Sand is tiny pieces of shells and **rocks / plastic**.

4 **Look and number. Then, match.**

First   Next   Then   Finally

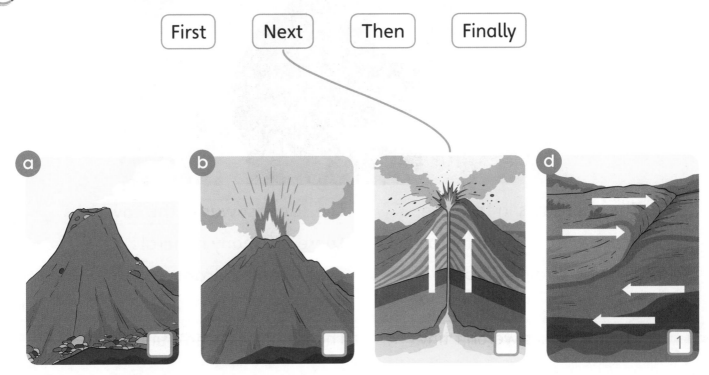

5 **Read and write the sequence words.**

The ocean makes sand! 1_____, the ocean waves hit rocks along the shore. 2_____Next_____, the big rocks break down into small rocks. 3_____, the small rocks break down into tiny rocks. 4_____, the rocks are so tiny that they are not rocks. They are sand!

Past Simple: Affirmative and Negative with *to be*

The volcano was **active in the past.**
It wasn't **a dormant volcano.**
Some beaches were **big.**
They weren't **colorful.**

1 **Circle the sentences about the past.**

a The scientist is in the cave.   (The scientist was in the cave.)
b There were many minerals.   There are many minerals.
c That isn't volcanic rock.   That wasn't volcanic rock.
d It is ice.   It was ice.
e The ice pieces weren't tiny.   The ice pieces aren't tiny.

2 **Look and circle the words.**

a There **was** / **were** many sea animals.
b Many of them **wasn't** / **weren't** small.
c This animal **was** / **were** a gigantic fish.
d It **was** / **were** a good swimmer.
e Some fish **wasn't** / **weren't** so strong.
f They **was** / **were** scared of the giant!

3 **Look and write.**

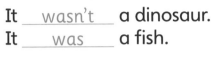
was   wasn't   were   weren't

> Look! These are animal fossils. These animals lived on Earth in the past.

a
It ___wasn't___ a dinosaur.
It ___was___ a fish.

b
They _____ butterflies.
They _____ ants.

c
They _____ fish.
They _____ dinosaurs.

d
It _____ a turtle.
It _____ a fish.

e
It _____ a bird.
It _____ a snake.

4 **Look and write the sentences.**

a

He / on a mountain ✓
He was on a mountain.

b

They / in the ocean ✗
_____

c

She / in a cave ✓
_____

d

It / in a river ✗
_____

My Life

Write about yourself in the past.

In the past,

I was _____ .

I wasn't _____ .

1 Circle the words that have the same sound as *ee* in *deep*.

1

(Deep) in the sea
there are three green fish.
Can you see them
around the reef?

2

Pete sits on the beach
next to a tall tree.
He sees a big bee
and jumps into the sea!

2 Color the pictures for the words that have the same sound as *deep*.

 deep

 fish

 shell

 beach

 bee

 sea

 sit

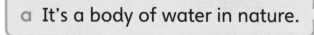 green

3 Complete with words that have the same sound as *ee* in *deep*.

clean   ~~sea~~   tree

a

b

c

What can you see
so close to the ___sea___?

There is just one bee
in that big _____!

The river looks green
when it's so _____!

Oracy

1 Read and match.

1 I don't understand.

2 Can you repeat that?

3 What is a river?

a It's a body of water in nature.

b Listen. I can explain again.

c Yes, I can.

68

Improve Your Writing

Improve Your Writing: Subject-Verb Agreement

The subject and verb of a sentence must agree. That means that when a subject is singular, the verb is singular.
The ladybug is small and shiny. **It**'s red and has black dots.

And, when the subject is plural, the verb is plural.
Ladybugs are good for the flowers. **Ladybugs** are beautiful, too.

1. **Read and color the turtle. Then, underline the plural subjects and the plural verbs in green.**

My Favorite Animal

By Said

I love turtles! A turtle is green and brown. It has a long neck and a small head. Turtles live in water and on land. They are quiet and slow. They eat insects and small fish. They can swim.

I think turtles are beautiful!

2. **Read and circle the correct answers.**

a What color is a turtle?

It's red and brown.   They are green and brown.   (It's green and brown.)

b What does a turtle's neck look like?

Turtle's necks are short.   Turtle's necks are small.   It's neck is long.

c What do turtles eat?

They eat insects and fish.   They eat eggs.   It eats chicken.

d What can they do?

They can run.   They can swim.   It can jump.

e What does Said think about turtles?

It is beautiful.   They are green.   They are beautiful.

1 READ **Look at the description on SB page 81. Complete the sentences.**

a A ladybug is red with __black__ spots.

b It is small and _____.

c It has _____ to fly.

d Ladybugs live in _____.

e They are _____ for the flowers.

f They _____ tiny insects.

My Favorite Animal
By Amy

I love ladybugs! A ladybug is red with black spots. It's small and shiny. It has wings. It can fly.

Ladybugs live in gardens. Ladybugs are good for the flowers. They eat tiny insects.

I think ladybugs are amazing!

2 PLAN **What is your favorite animal? Complete the chart.**

What is it?	What does it look like?	Where does it live?	What do they eat?	What can they do?	What do you think about it?

3 WRITE **Write a description of your favorite animal. Draw.**

My Favorite Animal By _____

_____

_____

_____

_____

4 EDIT **Check** ✓.

WRITING CHECKLIST

☐ I wrote about my favorite animal.

☐ I included information about its color, size, food, home, and special abilities.

☐ I used correct subject-verb agreement.

Ready to Read: Fiction

1 **Key Words 4** **Write the words in the puzzle.**

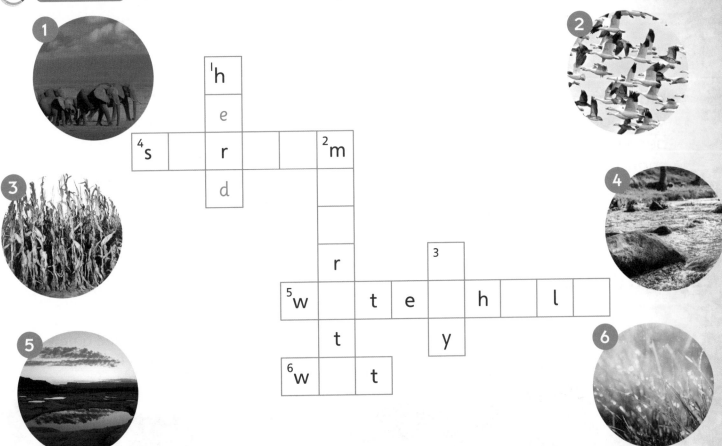

2 **Use words from Activity I to complete the sentences.**

> Our planet changes in many different ways.

a Animals can drink water from a ___stream___ or a _____.

b When it rains, the ground is _____.

c Fields are _____ when there isn't any rain.

d When there isn't any water or food, animals _____.

e Some animals travel in a group called a _____.

Reading Strategy: Summarizing

A summary is a short version of a text. It includes the main idea.

1 **Read and circle the best summary.**

Many things happen on our planet. Volcanoes erupt, and then they become dormant. The weather changes. New lakes and rivers form. Some lakes and rivers become dry. Animals and plants live and die.

a Animals and plants change.

b Some volcanoes change on our planet.

c On our planet, things are always changing.

d The weather sometimes changes.

2 **Read the story.**

A Safe Home

Sab and his family lived happily in a big forest. There was a lot of rain and many green trees. There was a stream in the forest, too.

There were many fish in the stream. There were a lot of birds in the trees. The air was clean, and the ground was wet. Sab and his family drank water from a big waterhole.

We need a new home. Let's find one!

One day, there wasn't any rain. There weren't any green trees. The waterhole was dry. There wasn't any food for Sab and his family. They were not safe!

They took their things and started walking. They walked for a long time.

Look! Here's a beautiful place! I like it!

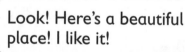

Sab and his family have a new home. There is a stream and green trees. There are birds and fish, too. It's a nice place!

(3) Circle Yes or No.

a At first, Sab and his family lived in a forest. (Yes) No

b First, the forest was dry. Yes No

c Then, there wasn't any water in the forest. Yes No

d Sab and his family moved. Yes No

e Now they are in another forest. Yes No

f They live on a beach. Yes No

(4) Circle the correct summary.

a Sab and his family lived happily in the dry forest.

b Sab and his family lived happily in the safe green forest.

a Sab and his family weren't safe because there wasn't any food or water.

b Sab and his family weren't safe because there were other animals.

a Sab and his family migrated to find a good place to live.

b Sab and his family planted more trees in the forest.

a Now Sab and his family are in a beautiful home that is not safe.

b Now Sab and his family are in a beautiful safe home.

(5) Complete the summary of the story *A Safe Home*.

First   safe   ~~happily~~   migrated   water   different

Sab and his family lived 1___happily___ in the forest. 2_____ , the forest was a safe place, but one day it was 3_____ . There wasn't any rain. There wasn't any 4_____ or food. Sab and his family 5_____ to a new place. They are now on a beautiful beach. There is a lot of water and food. They are in a 6_____ place again.

Past Simple *to be*, Yes/No Questions

Was the herd in the forest? Yes, it was. / No, it wasn't.
Were the waterholes dry? Yes, they were. / No, they weren't.

1 Look and match.

 **1** Was the dinosaur big?

 **2** Were the children in the library?

 **3** Was the boy scared?

 **4** Was the fish big?

 **5** Was she happy?

a ☐ No, it wasn't.

b ☐ Yes, she was.

c ☐ No, they weren't.

d ☐1 Yes, it was.

e ☐ No, he wasn't.

2 Unscramble the questions. Then, write the answers.

a Was / sleeping / the volcano / ?

Was the volcano sleeping?

No, it ____wasn't____ .

b the dinosaurs / around it / Were / ?

_____

Yes, they _____ .

c on fire / Were / the trees / ?

_____

No, they _____ .

d Was / red / the sky / ?

_____

Yes, it _____ .

74

3) Complete the questions. Then, circle the answers.

Was   Were | he   she   it   they

Hello!

a <u>Was he</u> on a tree?

Yes, he was.   (No, he wasn't.)

b _____ thirsty?

Yes, it was.   No, it wasn't.

c _____ a scientist?

Yes, she was.   No, she wasn't.

d _____ sad?

Yes, they were.   No, they weren't.

4) Look and write questions about the past.

shell / on the beach

<u>Was the shell on</u>
<u>the beach?</u>

dinosaurs / gigantic

_____

_____

they / big

_____

that turtle / old

_____

_____

My Life

Write questions to ask a member of your family about their past. Then, answer.

a Were you _____ ?

_____

b Were you _____ ?

_____

1 **Match the natural events with the related situations**

2 **Color the expressions about prevention.**

Let's recycle!

Throw that garbage in the lake!

Put this plastic in that special bin!

I never see red flags.

Let's plant one more tree!

I will wear my pajamas in the rain!

3 **Draw yourself taking action to prevent a disaster or problem.**

Check Your Oracy!

Read and circle *Yes* or *No*.

1 I gave my opinion. **Yes / No**

2 I asked questions when I didn't understand. **Yes / No**

The Big Challenge

 **Color** 😊 **or** 🙁 .

How can we make a 3D landscape?

We drew our landscape with rivers, volcanoes, mountains, and hills.	😊 🙁
We glued our landscape on a piece of cardboard.	😊 🙁
We pressed modeling clay onto the map to show the features.	😊 🙁
We presented our 3D landscape to the class.	😊 🙁

The Big Question and **Me**

Think and mark ✓. In Unit 4, I learned …

☐ a to talk about how our planet changes.

☐ b that prevention is important.

☐ c that some animals migrate when the landscape changes.

(1) Number the picture.

1 river

2 volcano

3 mountain

4 waterhole

5 cornfield

6 beach

(2) Look and complete the words.

a

R <u>a</u> i <u>n</u> fell on the h <u>i l l</u>.

b

The h__r__ was at the s__r____m.

c

There's a f__r__ by the l____e.

d

I can see some c__a c__s in the d__y ground.

(3) Complete the sentences.

~~shakes~~ grow ash scientists migrate

a The ground ____shakes____ before volcanoes erupt.

b Hot rocks and _____ come out of the volcano.

c Before this happens, some people _____ to be safe.

d _____ examine the rocks from volcanoes.

e Plants sometimes _____ on these rocks.

4 **Read and circle the correct words.**

a Some animals **was** / **were** at the waterhole.

b The land **wasn't** / **weren't** dry.

c There **was** / **were** many plants.

d The cornfield **was** / **were** green.

e Farmers **wasn't** / **weren't** sad.

5 **Complete the questions. Then, write the answers.**

Was   Were   Yes, it was.   No, it wasn't.   Yes, they were.   No, they weren't.

____Was____ the stream between mountains?

Yes, it was.

_____ the bears in the water?

_____ the lake dry?

_____ the elephants thirsty?

6 **Circle the correct verbs.**

a Our planet **change** / **changes** in different ways.

b Volcanoes **have** / **has** eruptions.

c Plants and trees **grow** / **grows** fast.

d The weather **are** / **is** different now.

e Many animals usually **migrate** / **migrates**.

SPEAKING MISSION

1 **Look and match.**

1 umbrella
2 raincoat
3 jacket
4 sunglasses
5 sweatshirt
6 shorts

a  ☐

b  ☐

c  ☐ 1

d  ☐

e  ☐

f  ☐

2 **Look and circle.**

a  It's rainy. Put on **(a raincoat)** / a hat.

b  It's sunny. Take **your jacket / your sunglasses.**

c  It's hot. Put on **a sweatshirt / a pair of shorts.**

d  It's cold. Put on **a jacket / a shirt.**

e  It's rainy. Take **a hat / an umbrella.**

3 **Number the dialogue lines in order.**

☐ It's cold. Put on a sweater.

1 Today is Friday, Mom. I want to play in the backyard.

☐ OK, Mom. Thanks!

☐ OK, let's put on some shorts.

☐ Great idea!

☐ It's sunny! Let's go to the park!

What can you remember about ... Unit 4?

1 Circle the words for a body of water.

lake   mountain   stream

volcano   river   waterhole

2 Unscramble the words.

hsake _____   rogw _____

3 What is this?

_____

4 Circle the correct words.

Was / Were the houses on the hill?

Yes, they **was / were**.

5 Who's looking for a tree to build a nest?

Enitan   Little Bird

6 Which two words have the same sound as *see*?

beach   reef   wet

7 Look and write the word.

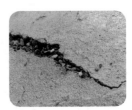

c __ a __ k

8 Look and complete the sentence.

He wants to be a _____ .

9 Number the words in order.

Next __   First __   Finally __

10 Unscramble the question.

the / Were / in the museum / children / ?

_____

Check your answers in the Student's Book. How did you do?
7–10 ☐ **Great!**   4–6 ☐ **Good!**   0–3 ☐ **Try harder!**

? 😀 How does our planet change?

81

5 What is music?

1 ▶ 5.1 **Watch the video. Complete the graphic organizer.**

Turkey   trumpet   Lucy   Morocco   guitar   Andy

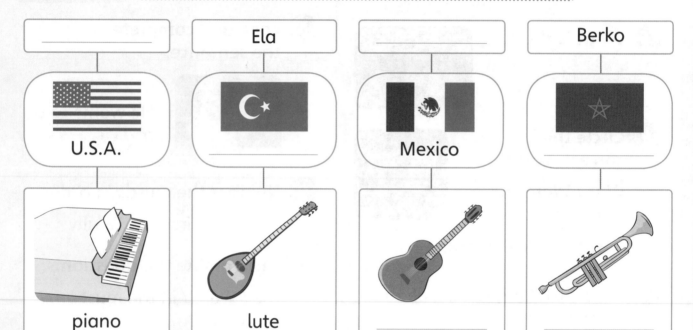

| _____ | Ela | _____ | Berko |

| U.S.A. | _____ | Mexico | _____ |

| piano | lute | _____ | _____ |

2 Key Words 1 **Complete the sentences.**

classical   piano   ~~folk~~   trumpet

 **a** Olga likes ___folk___ music. She plays and sings beautiful songs.

 **b** Adam and his sister take lessons in the afternoon. They enjoy _____ music.

 **c** Vick plays the _____ with his cousin Sasha.

 **d** Look at Tony and his music teacher. They play the _____.

Ready to Read: Nonfiction

1 Key Words 2 **Unscramble the letters and write the words. Then, match the words to the pictures.**

1 (opuparl) _____

a

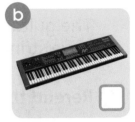
b

2 (potisioncom) _____

c

3 (ioviln) _____

d

4 (lchdi) _____

e

5 (oabrdeyk) _____

f

6 (hcri) _____

g

7 (rnea) _____

2 **Complete the sentences. Use words from the box.**

> child   compositions   keyboard   violin   popular

a When Mozart was a _____ , he played the piano.

b A lot of Mozart's music is very _____ today, too.

c Jaidynn Tyler is a boy from the United States. He plays the _____ very well.

d Alma Deutscher is an English girl. She plays the _____ .

e Alma writes musical _____ , too.

Reading Strategy: Rereading a Text

Sometimes you need to read a text more than once. Each time you read a text, you understand it better.

(1) **Read and circle the words for musical instruments.**

The guitar, the violin, and the lute are similar. They are made of wood and have strings. Some musicians play folk music with these instruments.

(2) **Reread the sentences and underline a kind of music.**

(3) **Read the text.**

Musical Instruments

Guitars, violins, and lutes are stringed instruments. A violin has four strings. To play a violin, musicians use a long, thin piece of wood called a bow. They move the bow against the strings to make music. A guitar has six strings, and a lute has 15 or 24 strings! Musicians can play the guitar and lute with their fingers.

Pianos and keyboards are percussion instruments. A piano has 88 keys. There are 52 white keys and 36 black keys. On a small keyboard, there are 25 keys. A big keyboard has 88, like a piano! Pianos and keyboards can make loud sounds or soft, quiet sounds.

Trumpets and flutes are wind instruments. Musicians blow into a trumpet or a flute to make music. Trumpets can make very loud sounds. Flutes make a softer, sweeter sound. Which instrument would you like to play?

(4) **Write the words.**

a A violin, a _____ , and a lute have strings.

guitar   trumpet

b A _____ has six strings.

violin   guitar   lute

c Pianos and keyboards are _____ instruments.

percussion   wind

d Trumpets and flutes are _____ instruments.

stringed   wind

e Flutes make _____ sounds.

loud   soft

(5) **Reread the text and complete the sentences.**

88 I5 36 24 25 52

a There are ____ or ____ strings on a lute.

b A piano has ____ black keys.

c A small keyboard has ____ keys.

d There are ____ white keys on a piano.

e A big keyboard has ____ keys.

(6) **Reread the text and complete the word.**

Musicians use a _____ to play the violin.

Past Simple Irregular Verbs

Mozart wrote **classical music.**
My classmates sang **a beautiful song.**
They had **some musical instruments.**

1 **Color the matching boxes.**

have   are   is   shake   sing   write

shook   had   wrote   sang   was   were

2 **Transform the sentences to past.**

a The composer writes the songs. _____

b The musicians have a big show. _____

c They are popular with children. _____

d The children sing loudly. _____

e One of them shakes a maraca. _____

f It is a great day. _____

3 **Write the verbs in past simple.**

make   go   grow   is   draw

This is Lorena.
She's a Mexican
folk singer.

a

Lorena _____ up in a
traditional Mexican
family.

b

Her grandmother _____
a popular musician.

c

Her grandfather _____
wooden musical
instruments, too.

d

Lorena always _____ to
traditional celebrations
with her grandparents.

e

Then, she _____
pictures of her family at
those celebrations.

4 **Circle the correct form of the verb.**

a Bells **are** / **were** very old musical instruments.

b A long time ago, people **make** / **made** the first bells.

c First, they **shake** / **shook** bells to call people.

d Then, they **play** / **played** music with them.

e Today a bell **is** / **was** usually a musical instrument.

My Life

Write about yourself.

Yesterday in school, I drew _____.

I wrote _____ .   I had _____.

Phonics

1 **Circle the words that have a long *u* sound.**

Playing music
is so cool!
Playing music
at home and at school!

One and two,
a new tune!
Three and four,
just for you!

2 **Color the words that have the same sound as *cool*.**

| two | you | three | four |

| new | now | go | school |

| rode | blue | home | music |

| cool | one | so | tune |

3 **Complete the rhymes.**

school   blue   new

a
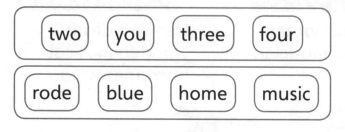

Those sounds are a few
and they are all _____ !

b

I want one or two of those
lutes that are _____ !

c
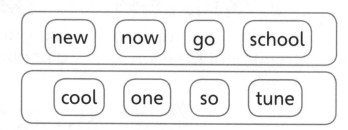

The music room in our
_____ is always so cool!

Oracy

1 **Read and match.**

a How about playing the guitar?

b Let's listen to classical music.

c How about singing some folk music?

Great! I love Mozart.

I know a Russian song.

Well, I'd like to play the piano.

Improve Your Writing: Types of Sentences

Affirmative: Chopin was born in Poland.
Negative: He wasn't very healthy.
Interrogative: Who was Chopin?
Exclamatory: He wrote music when he was seven!

1 **Read more about Chopin. Then, answer the questions.**

Who was Frédéric Chopin? He was a pianist and composer.
Chopin was born in Poland. He played the piano beautifully.
He wrote music when he was seven years old! He wasn't
very healthy. He was often sick. But he traveled around
Europe. He wanted everyone to hear his music!

a Who was Frédéric Chopin?   a teacher   a pianist

b Was Chopin healthy?   Yes, he was.   No, he wasn't.

c What did he do at seven years old?   He wrote music!   He played violin!

d Why did Chopin travel around Europe? _____

2 **Circle the sentences.**

affirmative ✏   negative ✏

interrogative ✏   exclamatory ✏

a Chopin was a pianist.

b He played the piano beautifully.

c What was special about Chopin?

d He wrote compositions when he was very young!

e Chopin didn't play the violin.

Writing

1 **READ** **Look at the biography on SB page 103. Circle the answers and underline the verbs.**

a Frédéric Chopin was born in …

Poland   France

b He was born in …

1810   1849

c He died in …

1810   1849

d He was a pianist and …

teacher   composer

Frédéric Chopin

• Who was Frédéric Chopin? Chopin was a famous pianist and composer.

• He was born in 1810 in Poland. He started composing music when he was seven years old!

• Chopin wrote many beautiful piano concertos. He didn't write any violin concertos.

• He died in France in 1849.

---

2 **PLAN** **Think of someone you admire. Complete the chart.**

Name: _____			
Born in (place)	Born in (year)	Died in (year)	Talents
_____	_____	_____	_____

3 **WRITE** **Write a biography of someone you admire.**

_____ was born in (place) _____ in (year)

_____

_____

_____

4 **EDIT** **Check ✓.**

WRITING CHECKLIST

☐ I included where and when the person was born, when they died, and things that are special about them.

☐ I used past simple verbs.

☐ I used different types of sentences.

1 Key Words 4 **Circle and match. Then, write the words.**

a

b

c

_____

_____

_____

w e a k m e e t s i c k s l o w d a n g e r o u s l o u d

d

e

f

_____

_____

_____

I can play the violin!

2 **Use words from Activity I to complete the sentences.**

a These children _____ in the music room.

b Today Sonia is not in class. She is _____ at home.

c Ula's music isn't _____. I can't hear it.

d Aida's music was fast yesterday, but today it is _____.

91

Reading Strategy: Identifying the Theme

The theme is the main subject or topic of a text.

1 **What is the theme of the story *The Little Red Hen*?**

a Little Red Hen likes to make bread.

b Little Red Hen works very hard, so she can eat the bread.

c Little Red Hen has hungry chicks, so she makes bread.

2 **Read the story.**

Whale Music

"Be careful, Win. Stay near me. It's dangerous in the ocean," said Mother Whale.

"Don't worry, Mom! I'm strong. I can swim alone," said Win.

Win swam away from his mom. He swam very far. Then, he saw a cave. He swam into the cave. It was cold and dark. Win was scared. He was lost!

"Oh, no! What can I do now? I know! I will sing my family's song."

Outside the cave, Win's mom, brother, and sister heard music. "Listen! It's Win! He's singing our family song!"

They sang back to Win. Win heard them. He followed their music out of the cave! Win was very happy to see his family. He never swam far away from them again.

3 Number the story events.

a

b

c

d

4 Circle the theme of the story.

a Your family can take you to safe places.

b It is important to do what your mother says.

c Swimming into dark caves is scary for whales.

5 Mark the theme of the story.

A Safe Home

Sab and his family lived happily in the forest. The forest was a safe place, but one day it was dry. There was no rain. There wasn't any water or food. Sab and his family migrated to a new place. Now they live on a beautiful beach. There is a lot of water and food. They are in a safe place again.

a Families want to live in dangerous places.

b Families need to have a safe home.

c Families like to live on the beach.

Possessive Pronouns

This is **my** guitar. It is **mine**.
Whose trumpet is this? It is **their** trumpet. It is **theirs**.

1 **Circle the possessive pronouns.**

a I have a flute.
This flute is mine .

b We have some musical instruments. They are ours.

c You have a guitar.
This guitar is yours.

d She has a violin.
The violin is hers.

e He has a trumpet.
The trumpet is his.

f They have a music room. It is theirs.

2 **Circle the answers.**

a Whose keyboard is this?

It's theirs.
It's hers.

b Whose music is it?

It's mine.
It's ours.

c Whose violin is that?

It's hers.
It's his.

d Whose guitar is this?

It's hers.
It's his.

e Whose trumpet is this?

It's theirs.
It's yours.

3 **Rewrite the sentences.**

a

These are our guitars.

_____They're ours._____

_____

b

That is the teacher's keyboard.

_____

_____

c

This is your music room.

_____

_____

d

That is the boys' piano.

_____

_____

4 **Unscramble the questions. Then, answer.**

a Whose / is / flute / it / ?

_____

It's his .   It's hers.

b Whose / are / bells / they / ?

_____

They're yours.   They're mine.

c Whose / it / piano / is / ?

_____

It's mine.   It's theirs.

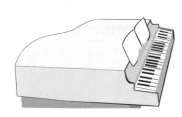

My Life

Draw pictures of two objects in your bedroom. Then, write the words.

a This _____ is mine.

b This _____ is mine, too.

1. **Match the pictures with the musical instruments.**

2. **Color the sentences that show appreciation for music.**

I like that sound.

I don't like it!

I like listening to those violins.

Folk music is beautiful!

Listen to this music!

I don't want to listen to it!

3. **Draw yourself appreciating music that you like.**

Check Your Oracy!

Read and circle _Yes_ or _No_.

1 I gave suggestions. **Yes / No**

2 I agreed and disagreed with my classmates. **Yes / No**

3 We made a plan. **Yes / No**

The Big Challenge

How can we appreciate music?

(1) **Color** **or** .

I closed my eyes and listened to three musical clips.	☺ ☹
I drew what I imagined.	☺ ☹
I discussed my feelings.	☺ ☹
I completed the sentence: _Because of music, I can ..._	☺ ☹
I made a poster.	☺ ☹
I presented my poster to the class.	☺ ☹

The Big Question and **Me**

Think and mark ✓**. In Unit 5, I learned ...**

☐ a to talk about musical instruments.

☐ b that it is important to appreciate music.

☐ c to use my imagination while listening to music.

1 **Write the words in the puzzle.**

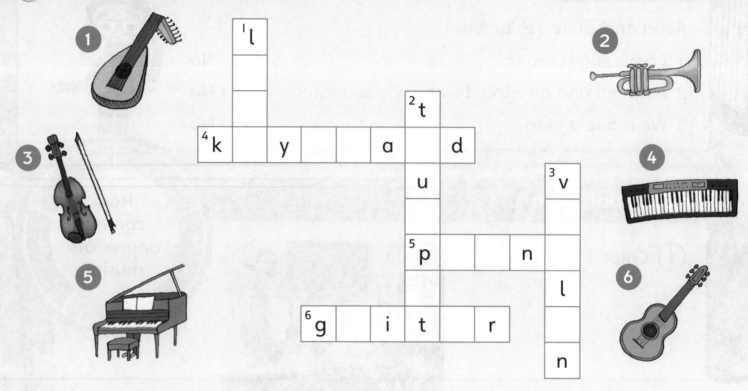

2 **Read and write the words.**

> weak   child prodigy   composition   classical music   musician   loud

a This is a musical creation: _____

b This person plays or makes music: _____

c This word is the opposite of *quiet*: _____

d Mozart wrote this kind of music: _____

e Chopin was this kind of child: _____

f This word is the opposite of *strong*: _____

3 **Read and circle the correct words.**

a Mozart was a **slow / popular** musician.

b He wasn't **rich / dangerous**.

c Chopin was **strong / sick** and died young.

d Some folk music is **safe / loud**.

e I'd like to **shake / meet** a musician.

4 **Circle the verbs in the past simple.**

a Mozart and Chopin **grow up / grew up** as child prodigies.

b They **write / wrote** beautiful classical music.

c They **were / are** popular.

d Chopin **is / was** very sick.

e Mozart's sister **was / is** a musician, too.

5 **Look and match.**

Whose violins are they?

1 It's mine.   2 That violin is his.   3 It's hers.   4 Those violins are theirs.

a   b   c   d

6 **Number the sentences.**

Affirmative = 1   Negative = 2   Interrogative = 3   Exclamatory = 4

a ☐ Music is loud or soft.

b ☐ Some people don't like folk music.

c ☐ Do they enjoy classical music?

d ☐ It's beautiful!

e ☐ What kind of music do you like?

SPEAKING MISSION

① Read, choose, and circle.

What kind of music is on your playlist?

rock and roll

classical

folk

pop

hip-hop

rap

country

jazz

② Write about yourself.

1 _____ music makes me feel relaxed.

2 I feel bored when I listen to _____ music.

3 _____ music makes me feel happy.

4 I feel sad when I listen to _____ music.

③ Number the dialogue lines in order.

3 What kind of music do you like?

☐ Good idea!

☐ How does it make you feel?

☐ I like pop music.

☐ Pop music makes me feel happy!

1 Let's make a playlist!

What can you remember about ... Unit 5?

1 **Circle the musical instruments.**

violin   popular   lute

composition   keyboard

2 **Match the opposites.**

dangerous   weak

strong   quiet

loud   safe

3 **What is this?**

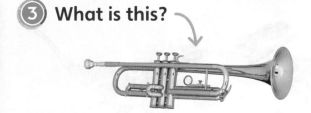

_____

4 **Complete the sentence.**

Mozart was a child

_____.

5 **Where was Mozart born?**

In Austria   in Germany

6 **Which two words have the same sound as _you_?**

blue   cool   slow

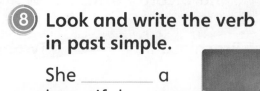

7 **Look and complete the words.**

f __ l k   m __ s ___ ___

8 **Look and write the verb in past simple.**

She _____ a beautiful song. (sing)

9 **Circle the correct word.**

The piano is **theirs / hers.**

10 **Unscramble the question.**

it / Whose / is / guitar / ?

_____

Check your answers in the Student's Book. How did you do?

7–10 ☐ Great!   4–6 ☐ Good!   0–3 ☐ Try harder!

? 😄 **What is music?** Circle.

6

What do we know about dinosaurs?

1 ▶ 6.1 **Watch the video. Complete the graphic organizer.**

~~enormous~~ carnivore long neck feathers carnivore
herbivore arms like wings sharp teeth chew meat

Brachiosaurus	**Tyrannosaurus Rex**	**Velociraptor**

enormous		

2 Key Words 1 **Complete the sentences.**

wings neck carnivore dinosaur herbivore chew

a The Brachiosaurus was an enormous
_____.

b It was a _____. It ate plants.

c It had a long _____ like a
giraffe's.

d The T-Rex was a _____. It could
_____ meat with its long, sharp
teeth.

e The Velociraptor's short arms looked like
a bird's _____.

SB pages 116–17

1 Key Words 2 **Complete the words. Then, number the pictures.**

1 f o _ _ i l

2 d _ _ _ _

3 m _ _ m _ l

4 h _ _ _ _

5 d _ _ t

6 c _ o _ d

a

b

c

d

e

f

2 **Complete the sentences.**

hit   fossils   extinction   mammals   dust

a Scientists study _____ to learn about the past.

b Dinosaurs and some _____ lived on Earth millions of years ago.

c Big rock pieces from volcanoes sometimes _____ animals and hurt them.

d There were big _____ clouds of dry sand when the wind was strong.

e What caused the _____ of the dinosaurs?

Reading Strategy: Main Idea and Details

The main idea is what the text is about. The details tell more about the main idea.

(1) Read and circle the main idea.

The T-Rex looked scary. It was a carnivore. It was a big, strong dinosaur with a very long tail. It had two short arms and two feet. It had long, sharp teeth to chew meat. The T-Rex ate other dinosaurs.

a The T-Rex was smaller than other dinosaurs.

b The T-Rex was dangerous to other dinosaurs.

c The T-Rex ran away from other dinosaurs.

(2) Read the text.

Ancient Creatures

Extinction!

Millions of years ago, dinosaurs became extinct. That means they all died. But why did they all die? There are many theories. About 65 million years ago, a giant rock called an asteroid hit Earth. It made a big dust cloud. It covered the planet.

Asteroid

There was no sunlight, so Earth got very cold. Many plants died, and there wasn't a lot of food. Then, the dinosaurs died. Many other animals died, too.

Animals that Survived!

Some animals did not die. We say that these animals survived. Amazing! Let's read about some of them.

Birds

Some scientists call birds living dinosaurs! These scientists studied many bird fossils. These fossils are millions of years old! The fossils show that birds were part of the dinosaur family. Dinosaurs are their ancestors.

Bird Fossil

Crocodiles

The ancestors of crocodiles lived 99 million years ago. Some of them were huge. The biggest one was 10 meters long—as long as a school bus!

Crocodile

Sea Turtles

The ancestors of sea turtles lived 90 million years ago. These sea turtles were giants. They were 4 meters long—as long as a car. There are sea turtles today, but they are smaller than their ancestors.

Sea Turtle

Cockroaches

Do you like cockroaches? Some people don't! Cockroaches are very, very old—their ancestors lived 150 million years ago. Cockroaches were also huge. There is a fossil of a cockroach that is 9 cm long!

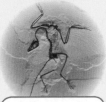

Cockroach

3 **Read the text again and circle the answers.**

a There is only one theory about how dinosaurs became extinct.   **Yes   No**

b A giant asteroid hit Earth about 65 million years ago.   **Yes   No**

c There was no sunlight after the asteroid hit.   **Yes   No**

d Dinosaurs are the ancestors of birds.   **Yes   No**

e The ancestors of crocodiles were smaller than crocodiles today. **Yes   No**

f There were sea turtles 150 million years ago.   **Yes   No**

g Survive means "to die."   **Yes   No**

4 **Circle two details for each main idea.**

Main idea 1: The dinosaurs and some other animals became extinct 65 million years ago.

Key details:

a A giant asteroid hit Earth. It made a giant dust cloud.

b The ancestors of crocodiles lived 99 million years ago.

c The dust cloud from the asteroid covered the sunlight. The Earth got very cold.

Main idea 2: Some animals survived the extinction 65 million years ago.

Key details:

a Ancestors of birds, crocodiles, sea turtles, and cockroaches lived millions of years before the asteroid hit Earth. They still live today.

b Scientists know how old the ancestors of these animals are from fossils.

c These animals were bigger millions of years ago.

5 **Number the events in order.**

☐ It got very cold.

☐ There was a giant dust cloud.

☐ The dinosaurs and many other animals died.

☐ Many plants died.

☐ The dust cloud covered the sunlight.

1 A giant asteroid hit the Earth 65 million years ago.

☐ There wasn't a lot of food to eat.

Past Simple Regular Verbs: Affirmative and Negative

Dinosaurs **lived** on Earth millions of years ago.
They **didn't survive** a natural disaster.

(1) **Color the matching boxes.**

lived

looked

watched

existed

died

played

didn't watch

didn't exist

didn't play

didn't live

didn't look

didn't die

(2) **Transform the sentences into the past simple.**

a Dinosaurs **live** on Earth.

_____

b Most of them **scare** other animals.

_____

c They **walk** around looking for food.

_____

d Some of them **move** slowly.

_____

e They **look** dangerous.

_____

f Others just **want** plants for food.

_____

③ Unscramble the sentences.

a The / studied / scientist / some fossils

_____

b These / many years ago / died / animals

_____

c them / The / showed / scientist / to me

_____

d liked / I / small fossils / the

_____

e in the ocean / These / lived / animals

_____

f didn't / They / scary / look

_____

④ Read and circle the correct verb in the present or past simple.

a Sharks **exist** / **existed** many years ago.

b They **didn't disappear** / **disappeared**.

c Ancient sharks **look** / **looked** enormous.

d Scientists now **call** / **called** ancient sharks Megalodons.

e Megalodons **don't move** / **didn't move** slowly.

f They **scare** / **scared** other ancient ocean animals.

My Life

Write about yourself.

> play talk look start work

Yesterday in school, …

I _____ .

I _____ .

I _____ .

1 **Read and circle** *t*, *d*, **or** *id*.

a
Did they exist?
Yes, they existed.
t   d   id

b
Did it happen?
Yes, it happened.
t   d   id

c
Did it start?
Yes, it started.
t   d   id

d
Did it stop?
Yes, it stopped.
t   d   id

e
Did it disappear?
Yes, it disappeared.
t   d   id

f
How did it look?
It looked sad!
t   d   id

2 **Color the boxes with the words that have the same sound as** *existed*.

started   worked   visited   looked   celebrated   opened

3 **Match the verbs that have the same sound.**

started   looked

happened   existed

stopped   disappeared

1 **Read and circle.**

a
That dinosaur is interesting.
Why?

Because we like it.
Because it can fly.

b
It's scary.
Why?

Because it has big teeth.
Because it can swim.

c
I think that dinosaur is hungry.
Why?

Because it wants to eat the rat.
Because it is running.

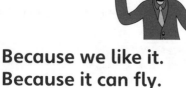

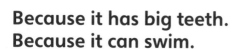

Improve Your Writing: Adjective Order

Adjectives normally go in the same order:

number ⟶ opinion ⟶ size ⟶ shape ⟶ color

two long horns   **one small round** turtle   a **scary green** dinosaur

1 **Read the Fact File. Circle the phrases with more than one adjective.**

Iguanodon (i-GUAN-o-don)

Diet: herbivore
Lived: 130 million years ago
Weight: 5,000 kg
Height: 2.7 meters
Length: 10 meters

Characteristics:
- two spiky thumbs
- a long, pointy tail
- a small, round head
- walked on two or four small feet

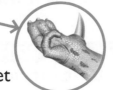

2 **Read and complete the chart.**

blue   scary   three   huge   pointy   yellow   65   delicious   tiny   round

Number	Opinion	Size	Shape	Color

3 **Write the adjectives in the correct order.**

a I gave my mom _____ flowers.   pretty two

b The scientists studied _____ fossils.   100 old

c The sea turtle has a _____ head.   round small

d My dog has _____ eyes.   big two brown

Writing

1 **READ** Look at the Fact File on SB page 125. Complete the sentences.

a The triceratops was a ___herbivore___. It ate plants.

b It lived _____ million years ago.

c It weighed 6,000 _____.

d It was _____ meters tall and 9 meters _____.

e It had a huge, _____ head.

f Its skin was _____.

Triceratops
(try-SER-a-tops)

Diet: herbivore

Lived: 68 million years ago

Weight: 6,000 kg

Height: 3 meters tall

Length: 9 meters long

Characteristics:
- walked on four short legs
- a huge, heavy head
- two long sharp horns on the head
- a long, thick tail
- one short horn on the nose
- thick skin

2 **PLAN** **WRITE** Complete a Fact File about your favorite dinosaur. Illustrate your Fact File.

Name: _____

Diet: _____

Lived: _____ million years ago

Weight: _____ kg

Height: _____ meters tall

Length: _____ meters long

Characteristics:

- _____
- _____
- _____
- _____

3 **EDIT** Check ✓.

WRITING CHECKLIST

☐ I wrote facts about my favorite dinosaur.

☐ I used short phrases and numbers.

☐ I used adjectives in the correct order.

Ready to Read: Fiction

1 Key Words 4 **Unscramble the words.**

a

rkda

_____

b

apht

_____

c

urfintuer

_____

d

roudng

_____

e

yadghtli

_____

f

ghtnitiem

_____

2 **Use words from Activity I to complete the sentences.**

a It was ___nighttime___ in the jungle.

b There were big rats on the _____ .

c A T-Rex walked down the _____ .

d The sky was

_____ .

It started raining!

Reading Strategy: Beginning, Middle, and End

Stories have three parts: a beginning, a middle, and an end.

1 **Look and number the beginning (I), the middle (2), and the end (3).**

I love this bed!

I can make a bed with this wood.

I want a new bed for my birthday.

2 **Read the story.**

Family History

Did our family walk in the past? Did we use wings to fly? Why did we grow a beak?

Because some things changed in our family a long time ago.

Why?

It was nighttime and Tiny had some questions for Grandma.

"Millions of years ago, your ancestors Rap and Tor lived on Earth. They had a big family and many friends.

Rap and Tor lived happily, but one day, a big volcano erupted! Rap and Tor saw the fire and ash. They were scared. They ran fast!

Rap and Tor climbed up a tall tree. They were safe! Then, they went to sleep.

When they woke up, everything was different. The volcano wasn't there! Rap and Tor had changed, too. Now they were birds!"

I like my wings. I can fly!

Look at my beak!

3 **Look and match.**

Did we use wings
to fly?

Did our family
walk in the past?

Why did we grow
a beak?

4 **Read and circle the correct words.**

a Rap and Tor lived **hundreds** / **millions** of years ago.

b They had a **big** / **small** family and lots of friends.

c A **volcano** / **asteriod** erupted.

d Rap and Tor ran fast and climbed a **mountain** / **tree**.

e Rap can use his wings to **eat** / **fly**.

5 **Number the beginning (I), middle (2), and end (3).**

a

Rap and Tor climbed up a tall tree. They were safe!
Then, they went to sleep.

b

One day, a big volcano erupted! Rap and Tor saw the
fire and ash. They were scared. They ran fast!

c

When they woke up, everything was different. Rap
and Tor had changed. Now they were birds! They flew
away.

Past Simple Regular Verbs: Questions

Did our family walk in the past? **Yes, they did.**
Did we use wings to fly? **No, we didn't.**
Why did they change? Because they needed to survive.

1 **Complete the questions.**

look   ask   walk   like   disappear   visit

a _____ you _____ the museum?
Yes, we did.

b _____ you _____ questions?
Yes, I did.

c _____ rats _____ from Earth?
No, they didn't.

d _____ that dinosaur _____ on four feet?
Yes, it did.

e _____ it _____ like a fish?
No, it didn't.

f _____ you _____ the fossil?
Yes, we did.

2 **Unscramble the questions and number the answers.**

1 Where / work / scientist / the / did / ?

_____

2 study / did / What / he / ?

_____

3 did / When / you / to him / talk / ?

_____

4 he / open / that box / did / Why / ?

_____

5 What / you / show / did / he / ?

_____

☐ He showed me some dinosaur bones.

☐ He studied history and nature.

☐ He worked at the museum.

☐ I talked to him yesterday.

☐ He wanted to show me a discovery.

3 Complete the questions.

When   Where   Why   What

a _____ did dinosaurs live?

They lived more than 130 million years ago.

b _____ did they live?

They lived in many places around the world.

c _____ did they like to eat?

Some were herbivores and others were carnivores.

d _____ did they disappear?

Scientists think that a big rock hit the earth.

4 Write questions about the ocean dinosaur.

Why / disappear   What / color
How many / feet   Where / live

a _____

b _____

c _____

d _____

My Life

Write three questions to ask your grandparents or a family member about the past.

1 What _____ ?

2 When _____ ?

3 Why _____ ?

1 Match the pictures with the different ways to learn about the past.

☐ reading books
☐ asking questions
☐ visiting museums
☐ using the Internet
☐ watching videos

2 Color the question words to learn about the past.

a (Numbers:)   (Why)   (How many)

b (Places:)   (Where)   (How)

c (People:)   (Who)   (What)

d (Reasons:)   (When)   (Why)

e (Time:)   (Where)   (When)

f (Actions or objects:) (What) (Why)

3 Draw yourself asking three questions to learn about the past.

Check Your Oracy!

Read and circle *Yes* or *No*.

1 I gave reasons to support my opinion.   **Yes / No**

2 I asked for reasons.   **Yes / No**

The Big Challenge

How can we learn about a dinosaur?

1 Color or .

I chose a dinosaur and did research.	☺ ☹
I wrote down some facts.	☺ ☹
I made a fact file.	☺ ☹
I drew a picture of the dinosaur.	☺ ☹
I presented my report to the class.	☺ ☹

The Big Question and **Me**

Think and mark ✓. In Unit 6, I learned …

☐ a to talk about dinosaurs.

☐ b that it is important to learn about the past.

☐ c to ask questions about the past.

(1) Complete the sentences.

carnivore   extinction   herbivore   furniture   chew   die

a A _____ eats plants.

b _____ is the opposite of *live*.

c _____ is the disappearance of animals or plants from Earth.

d A _____ eats meat.

e Carnivores _____ meat with their teeth.

f Tables and chairs are pieces of _____.

(2) Look and write the words.

1 c_____
2 w_____
3 d_____
4 p_____
5 m_____

(3) Read the questions and complete the answers.

a Why do we know about dinosaurs?   Because scientists study f __ s ___ l s.

b How did some herbivores eat leaves from tall trees?   They had long n __ c __ s.

c Why did dinosaurs disappear?   It's a m __ s __ e r __, but there is a theory.

d What's the theory?   A big rock h __ __ the earth.

e When did they find the fossil?   They found it at n __ g __ t t __ me.

4 **Read and circle the correct words.**

a In class we **talked / didn't talk** about dinosaurs.

b Different kinds of dinosaurs **lived / didn't live** on Earth in the past.

c Some dinosaurs were quick, but others **moved / didn't move** fast.

d Some of them ate meat, but others **liked / didn't like** it.

e They **survive / didn't survive** after the giant rock.

f They **died / didn't die**.

5 **Complete the questions about the past.**

a What color _____ you _____ your dinosaur? (paint)

b How many teeth _____ you _____? (count)

c _____ carnivores _____ food with those big teeth? (chew)

d When _____ they _____ on Earth? (live)

e _____ they _____ a long time ago? (disappear)

6 **Mark ✓ the adjectives in correct order.**

☐ a It had a __long, thick__ tail.

☐ b It was a __thin, short__ neck.

☐ c Did it have __two big__ ears?

☐ d That was a __green, beautiful__ dinosaur.

☐ e There were __three, scary__ animals.

1 Look and number.

1 jug of water   2 canned food   3 umbrella   4 sunscreen
5 flashlight   6 blanket   7 whistle   8 can opener

a  ☐

b  ☐

c  ☐

d  ☐

e  ☐

f  ☐

g  ☐

h  ☐

2 Match.

1 Let's bring a blanket.
2 Can you repeat that, please?
3 Why did you choose the umbrella?
4 It's necessary because it might rain.

a Asking for an explanation
b Making a suggestion
c Giving an explanation
d Asking for clarification

3 Number the dialogue lines in order.

1 What should we bring with us?
☐ Good idea! How about a can opener?
☐ Let's bring a flashlight and some canned food.
☐ Why do we need a can opener?
☐ Oh, yes, we need one!
☐ To open the cans.

SB pages 136–37

What can you remember about ... Unit 6?

1 Circle the parts of an animal's body.

dust   neck   chew

teeth   wing

2 Complete the words.

night_____   _____light

3 What is this?

It's a _____

4 Complete the sentence.

A _____ eats plants.

5 Circle the brachiosaurus.

a   **b**

6 Which word has the same sound as *invited*?

opened   stopped   painted

7 Look and complete the word.

e __ t i __ __ t i __ n

8 Circle the words.

Dinosaurs **lived / didn't live** on Earth millions of years ago.

They **survived / didn't survive** natural disasters.

9 Who lived in the cave Dina and Dino found?

_____

10 Unscramble the question.

did / Why / disappear / dinosaurs / ?

_____

Check your answers in the Student's Book. How did you do?

7–10 ☐ Great!   4–6 ☐ Good!   0–3 ☐ Try harder!

? 😄 What do we know about dinosaurs?

Carnivores had big _____ .

_____ ate plants.

Dinosaurs became extinct _____ of years ago.

(1) ▶ 7.1 **Watch the video. Complete the graphic organizer.**

Ecuador Canada baseball exercise cook Brazil

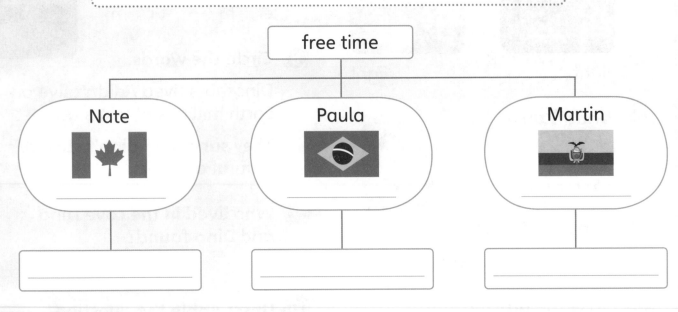

free time

Nate

Paula

Martin

_____

_____

_____

_____

_____

_____

(2) [Key Words 1] **Complete the sentences.**

watch baseball exercise cook play park

a

Nate and his team go to the _____. They play _____ there.

b

Paula stays at home to _____. She makes pies with her mom. Then, they _____ movies.

c

Martin likes being outdoors, too. He loves to _____ with his family. Then, they all _____ video games at home.

1 Key Words 2 **Circle the letters and write the words.**

a

b

c

d

dfateks   ledntrils   pykrabmids   tbootdhpavstie

_____   _____   _____   _____

e

f

g

laocmkub   mamrbples   gkaeyzs

_____   _____   _____

2 **Complete the sentences with words from Activity I.**

a Ancient Egyptians ate _____ at parties.

b They had honey and _____ for dessert.

c They built huge _____ thousands of years ago.

d They made small metal objects like locks and _____.

e Did ancient Egyptians use _____ to brush their teeth?

f Yes, they did, and children played with _____ and other toys we have today.

Reading Strategy: Summarizing

A summary is a short version of a text. It includes the main idea.

1 **Read and circle the best summary.**

Kites are ancient. They were invented in Asia a long time ago. Now there are kites all over the world. Kites are usually very colorful, and they are all different shapes and sizes. Some have tails, like this one. And some have special parts that make music! People use kites for fishing, sports, and games. People also use kites for festivals and celebrations. In Japan, some people fly kites that have the name of their new babies!

a People in ancient China invented kites.

b There are many different kites, and they are used for different reasons.

c Some kites have special parts that make music!

2 **Read the text.**

The Maya Civilization

Cities

The Maya lived in Mesoamerica thousands of years ago. This place is now Central America. The Maya lived in rainforests and jungles. They built cities with huge stone pyramids.

Special Game

The Maya people played a popular ball game called *Pok-A-Tok*. Players moved a ball through a stone ring, like basketball. They hit the ball with their heads, arms, or shoulders. They didn't use their hands or feet!

Stone Ring

Culture

The Maya were good at math, and they made a calendar. They were artisans, too. They used precious stones like jade to make masks and decorate their buildings. The Maya ate corn, beans, and sweet potatoes. They made flat corn pancakes called tortillas. They sometimes ate fish and meat. They also ate honey.

Beans

Tortillas

Jade

3 **Read and circle the words.**

a The Maya lived in Mesoamerica **millions** / **thousands** of years ago.

b This place is now **Central** / **North** America.

c The Maya built cities with **small** / **huge** stone pyramids.

d They used precious stones like jade to make **pyramids** / **masks**.

e The Maya made flat **potato** / **corn** pancakes called tortillas.

f To play *Pok-a-Tok*, the Maya hit the ball with their **hands** / **shoulders**.

4 **Read and mark ✓ the best summary for each paragraph.**

Cities

☐ a The huge pyramids in Mayan cities were made of stone.

☐ b The Maya built their cities in rainforests and jungles in Mesoamerica.

Culture

☐ a The Maya were good at math, ate many different kinds of food, and made crafts with jade.

☐ b The Maya made a calendar and some jade stone masks.

Special Game

☐ a When playing *Pok-A-Tok*, the Maya hit a ball with their heads, arms, and shoulders to get it through a stone ring.

☐ b The Maya didn't use their hands or feet when they played *Pok-A-Tok*.

5 **Read and write the words.**

a They were huge stone buildings: _____

b They used it to make masks: _____

c It was the name of the ball game: _____

Grammar in Context

1 **Color the matching boxes.**

fly   go   have

draw   eat

get   ride   see

ate   rode

had   saw   went   drew   got

flew

2 **Transform the sentences to past simple.**

a

Ancient people's celebrations **are** interesting.

b

The ancient Chinese **have** festivals.

c

They **make** musical instruments.

d

They **tell** stories.

e

Some of them **write** poems.

f

Others **wear** colorful costumes.

③ **Read and circle the verbs.**

Children in the past played hopscotch, too.

a They **drew / didn't draw** a hopscotch grid on the ground.

b They **wrote / didn't write** any letters. They wrote numbers.

c They hopped and **got / didn't get** to number ten.

d Then, they **went / didn't go** back to number one.

e They **won / didn't win** if they fell down!

④ **Complete the sentences.**

fly   tell   run   have   make   ride

> **What did ancient Chinese children do in their free time?**

a They _____ any computers.

b They _____ colorful kites.

c They sometimes _____ after each other to play tag.

d They _____ bikes, and they didn't watch movies.

e They _____ shadow puppets and _____ stories with them.

My Life

Write about yourself.

write   draw   sit   eat   see   ride   read

Yesterday in school, ...

✓ I _____ .

✗ I _____ .

✓ I _____ .

✗ I _____ .

1 **Read and circle the words with** *wh* **or** *ph*.

a Why are you whining?

b I can't find my photo!

c What's in that photo?

d A whale and an elephant!

e Look! Your photo!

f Where was it?

g Under that white graph!

2 **Circle the word that is different.**

a why	while	pharmacy
b photo	graph	white

c whale	elephant	where
d whine	photo	Phil

3 **Write** *wh* **or** *ph*.

a ____oto   b ____ale   c ele____ant   d gra____   e ____ite

1 **Read and match.**

a That's too fast.

b I can't hear.

c That's too slow!

☐ Speak up, please!

☐ Speak more quickly.

☐ Speak more slowly.

Improve Your Writing: Change Verbs to Show Time

You can talk about what is happening now: **I am read**ing.
You can talk about everyday actions: **I go to school every day.**
You can talk about the past: **I went to school yesterday.**

1 **Read the diary entry. Circle the verbs.**

Dear Diary,

Today is Sunday. I'm listening to music in my bedroom. It's raining now,
but it didn't rain this morning. My parents took Ula and me to the park.
We played baseball there. I was happy and had lots of fun. Then, we ate
lunch. Dad, Ula, and I had a sandwich, but Mom had some salad.

Right now, Ula is watching a movie. Mom and Dad are in the kitchen.
They always cook together. Right now, they're making dinner.
We always have dinner together, and we talk about our day!

Frida

2 **Color the boxes.**

past actions = ▬▬▶   actions now = ▬▬▶   everyday actions = ▬▬▶

| a It's **raining**. | b They always **cook** together. | c Ula **is watching** a movie. |

| d Then, we **ate** lunch. | e We **talk** about our day. |

| f It **didn't rain** this morning. |

3 **Complete the sentences.**

play   watching   skating   ride   rained

a I'm _____ TV in my bedroom.

b We _____ the bus to school every day.

c My friend and I _____ video games after school.

d My brother is _____ right now.

e It _____ yesterday.

Writing

(1) READ Look at the diary entry on SB page 147. Check ✓ or put an ✗.

a ☐ It was Monday.

b ☐ She ate a small breakfast.

c ☐ The friends went to the pool and ate ice cream.

d ☐ The ice cream was delicious.

e ☐ It was a bad day.

Dear Diary,

Today was Saturday, so there was no school. Yay!

I woke up late, took a shower, and got dressed.

Then, I ate a big breakfast: three pancakes, one banana, and a chocolate smoothie!

I usually eat a very small breakfast. I eat cereal with milk.

At 10 a.m., my two best friends came over. We swam at the pool in the park. It was really fun! Then, we went out for ice cream. I had strawberry ice cream. It was delicious!

Right now, I am lying on my bed. I'm watching my favorite movie on my tablet. It's so funny! It's making me laugh!

Today was a great day!

(2) PLAN Complete the chart.

What Day Is It?	What I Did Today	How I Felt

(3) WRITE Write a diary entry about your day.

Dear Diary,
Today is _____

_____

_____

_____

_____

(4) EDIT Check ✓.

WRITING CHECKLIST

☐ I included the day.

☐ I wrote about what I did and how I felt.

☐ I used verbs for the past, now, and everyday actions correctly.

(1) **Key Words 4** **Circle six words. Then, label the pictures.**

a

broken

j	u	p	c	b	r	o	b	o	t	m	a	y
k	f	r	a	l	p	c	t	u	w	n	e	t
o	i	n	s	t	r	u	c	t	i	o	n	s
p	x	o	p	w	n	v	a	y	z	d	u	i
r	o	l	e	q	h	b	r	c	a	b	l	e
t	m	t	a	u	s	a	t	i	u	s	l	n
b	r	o	k	e	n	e	o	l	o	u	m	d

b

c

d

e

I'm a robot!

f

USER MANUAL

(2) **Use words from Activity I to complete the sentences.**

a Our robot is _____ .

b We can _____ it!

c We read the _____ on the tablet.

d We need some _____ .

e Now we have a new _____ .

f It can move, but it can't _____ !

131

Reading Strategy: Text-to-Self Connection

When you read a text, you can make a connection between the text and your life or experiences.

① Read and mark ✓ what you do with your family.

My name is Gabe and this is my family. We usually go camping. Look at our blue tent! When we go camping, we eat sandwiches and fruit. We play board games together, and we read stories at nighttime. We sometimes take long walks, too.

☐ go camping
☐ play board games
☐ read stories
☐ take long walks

② Read the story.

The Flying Robot

It was Saturday. Burak and his sister Esma were bored. "We can't play outside. It's raining!"

They played video games and board games in the living room.

Finally, they took out a big box. They painted it yellow and green. Then, they put some red wings on it.

It looks like a flying robot!

It is a speaking robot. Look!

My name is Robby. I can speak. I can fly. I can take you anywhere! Hop in!

It's time for dinner!

I am broken now. Let's land! You have to fix me. Listen to my instructions!

Burak and Esma followed the robot's instructions. They fixed its cables.

That was fun!

3 **Draw your robot. What does it look like?**

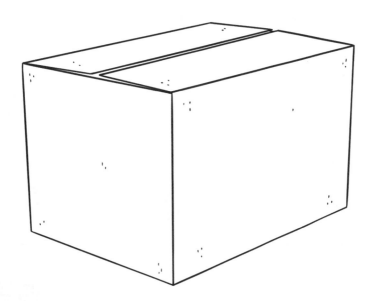

My robot is **big / small**. It has **eyes / arms / wings / wheels**. It can _____.

4 **Read the story again and circle _Yes_ or _No_.**

a	It was Sunday.	Yes	No
b	Burak and his sister Esma were bored.	Yes	No
c	They played video games and watched a movie.	Yes	No
d	The flying robot talked to Burak and Esma.	Yes	No
e	Burak and Esma fixed the robot.	Yes	No
f	It was time for lunch.	Yes	No

5 **Circle what you like to do in your free time.**

a I play outside.

b I play video games.

c I play inside when it's raining.

d I play board games.

e I use my imagination to play.

Past Simple Irregular Verbs: *Wh-* Questions

Why did **it** fly? Because it had **wings.**
What did **they** read? They read **the instructions.**

1 **Complete the questions.**

> Who   When   Where   Why   What

a _____ did she do? She wrote a diary entry.

b _____ did she sit? She sat under a tree.

c _____ did she write it? She wrote it in the morning.

d _____ did she write the diary entry? Because she had a great day.

e _____ read her diary? Nobody read her diary.

2 **Unscramble the questions and number the answers.**

1 Where / go / they / did / ?

_____

2 see / did / What / they / ?

_____

3 did / What time / they / eat / ?

_____

4 they / come back / did / When / ?

_____

5 Why / they / like / did / the forest / ?

_____

☐ They saw some animals.

☐ They came back at 5:00.

☐ They went to the forest.

☐ Because it was interesting.

☐ They ate at 12:00.

3) **Write the questions in the past simple and complete the answers.**

Where / you / go?

_____

I _____ to the toy store.

What / they / choose?

_____

They _____ a robot.

c Hello!

What / it / do?

_____

It _____ English.

d day | Tuesday | V

When / they / buy it?

_____

They _____ it on Tuesday.

4) **Write questions in the past simple about a family trip.**

> Where / go   What / do   When / come back

Yesterday my family and I went on a trip.

a _____

b _____

c _____

My Life

Write three questions about your parents' past free-time activities.

a What _____ ?

b When _____ ?

c Where _____ ?

(1) Number the free-time activities.

- [ ] swimming
- [ ] camping
- [ ] baking
- [ ] reading
- [ ] running
- [ ] ice skating

(2) Complete the sentences with a free-time activity.

1 _____ is fun.

2 _____ is interesting.

3 _____ is exciting.

4 _____ is boring.

5 _____ is my favorite free-time activity.

(3) Draw yourself doing your favorite free-time activity.

Check Your Oracy!

Read and circle *Yes* or *No*.

1 I spoke clearly and at the right pace. **Yes / No**

2 My classmates asked me to speak up. **Yes / No**

The Big Challenge

(1) **Color** **or** ☹ .

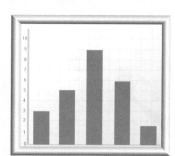

How can we make a survey?

I wrote a list of five free-time activities.	☺ ☹
I made a chart.	☺ ☹
I asked ten classmates if they did those activities.	☺ ☹
I made a graph with the answers.	☺ ☹
I reported my findings to the class.	☺ ☹

The Big Question and **Me**

Think and mark ✓. In Unit 7, I learned …

☐ a to talk about free-time activities.

☐ b that free-time activities are important.

☐ c to ask questions about the past.

(1) Complete the sentences.

speak   fix   exercise   watch   invent

a We can _____ in the school gym.

b Some scientists _____ machines.

c The tablet is broken and we can't _____ it.

d In our free time, we _____ movies.

e Do you _____ English?

(2) Look and complete the sentences.

a Ancient Egyptians built _____.

b They used _____ to brush their teeth.

c They invented the lock and _____.

d Egyptian children played with _____.

e They ate dates and _____.

(3) Read and complete the paragraph.

responsibility   park   instructions   baseball

I work in this place. Many children come to this 1_____ in their free time. Some of them play 2_____, and others ride their bikes. It's important for them to follow my 3_____. Taking care of the park is my 4_____.

7

4 **Read and circle the correct verb.**

a On Friday we **rode** / **didn't ride** our bikes. ✗

b We **wrote** / **didn't write** some stories. ✓

c Then, we **went** / **didn't go** to the park. ✓

d We **saw** / **didn't see** any birds there. ✗

e Our friends **left** / **didn't leave** early. ✓

f They **ate** / **didn't eat** dinner with us. ✗

5 **Complete the questions.**

> What   Where   When   Why   What

a _____ did you go? We went to the park.

b _____ did you do there? We played hopscotch.

c _____ didn't you swim? Because it was too cold.

d _____ did you go back home? In the afternoon.

e _____ did you do then? We watched a movie.

6 **Circle the correct sentences.**

Yesterday

a I'm drawing a treehouse.   b I drew a treehouse.

Now

a They're reading a story.   b They read a story.

Usually

a We take long walks.   b We took a long walk.

SPEAKING MISSION

1 **Look and number. Then, circle the activities you chose for your Speaking Mission.**

1 watch videos online

2 play the piano

3 swim

4 go fishing

5 climb trees

6 collect insects

2 **Read and match the questions and answers.**

1 What do you want to do?

2 Where can we go fishing?

3 When can we do it?

4 What do we need?

☐ We can do it in the morning.

☐ Let's go fishing!

☐ We need a fishing pole.

☐ How about the lake?

3 **Number the dialogue lines in order.**

☐ What do we need?

☐ Good idea! Where do you want to do that?

1 What do you want to do on Saturday morning?

☐ Let's go swimming.

☐ How about the pool?

☐ We need our swimsuits.

What can you remember about ... Unit 7?

① Circle two kinds of food.

toothpaste   key   lentils

lock   dates

② Unscramble the words.

bclae _____   rmalbe _____

③ What is this?

_____

④ Complete the sentence.

Playing _____ is fun.

⑤ Circle the lock.

⑥ Which word has the same sound as *whale*?

elephant   graph   white

⑦ Complete the word.

r e s __ o n s __ b i l i t __

⑧ Circle the correct verbs.

We **eat / ate** vegetables every day.

They **don't fly / didn't fly** their kites yesterday.

⑨ What was Brad's robot's name?

_____

⑩ Unscramble the question.

did / What / draw / you / ?

_____

Check your answers in the Student's Book. How did you do?
7–10 ☐ Great!   4–6 ☐ Good!   0–3 ☐ Try harder!

? 😊 Why is free time important?

Free time is important to relax and have a good time with your _____ and family.

8

What is a hero?

1 ▶ 8.1 **Watch the video. Complete the graphic organizer.**

brave   caring   generous   helpful   help   takes care of   collects   saves

and _____
people in danger

and gives time
to _____
nature

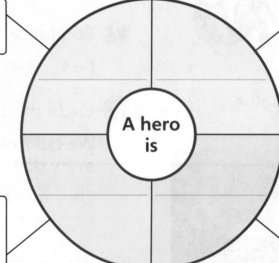

A hero
is

and _____
children in
hospitals

and _____
trash

2 Key Words 1 **Complete the sentences.**

hero   brave   save   generous   caring

a

A firefighter is
_____. He can
_____ people
and animals from
danger.

b

A _____
person likes giving.
You can be a
_____ when
you give others what
they need.

c

Doctors and nurses
are helpful and
_____. They
work with people
in hospitals to help
them feel better.

SB pages 160–161

1 Key Words 2 **Circle and write the words.**

h e a l t h y b l i n d t r a i n s m a r t s c e n t h e a v y d e p r e s s e d

a

b

c

_____

_____

_____

_____

e

f

g

_____

_____

_____

2 **Complete the sentences. Use words from Activity I.**

a Animals are _____ heroes that help people to do things better.

b A dog's nose has around 300 million _____ receptors, so people can _____ them to look for lost people and objects.

c Guide dogs help _____ people to go around the city.

d Scientists say that having a pet can help sick people feel _____ again.

e Having a cat as a pet can make _____ people happy.

f Some animal heroes, like horses and donkeys, carry _____ loads from one place to another.

Reading Strategy: Captions

The sentences or phrases under a picture can give you more information about the text.

1 Look and circle the captions.

a

Police train dogs to save people in danger.

Police train dogs to be good pets at home.

b

Generous man gives a sandwich to a hungry boy.

Generous boy gives a sandwich to a hungry man.

2 Read the text and circle the three captions.

Real-Life Heroes

Vets

Vets are generous and caring heroes. They help sick animals feel healthy again. They sometimes rescue animals in danger, too. Sometimes they help animals find homes. Vets know that pets can help people feel better.

Vet taking care of kitten

Firefighters

Firefighters are heroes. They risk their lives to save people and sometimes animals, too. They wear heavy boots and a special coat and hat for protection. Firefighters practice running and climbing fast. They can put out fires in buildings and forests. They help take people out of buildings on fire, too. Firefighters sometimes go to schools and teach children how to be safe from fires.

Doctors

Doctors are very special heroes. They work in hospitals to help people who are sick. They help them to feel better. Sometimes doctors travel very far to help sick people. Doctors do many things to help people feel better but it isn't an easy job!

Firefighter with children in school

Doctor talking to girl in a hospital

3 Mark ✓ the statements.

✓firefighters   ✓vets   ✓doctors

a They know that pets can help people feel better.   ☐

b They wear heavy boots and a special coat and hat for protection.   ☐

c Sometimes they help animals find homes.   ☐

d They do many things to help people feel better.   ☐

e They practice running and climbing fast.   ☐

f They sometimes travel very far to help sick people.   ☐

g They go to schools to talk about how to stay safe from fires.   ☐

4 Complete the sentences with words from the text.

a Firefighters can put out ___forest___ fires.

b They save _____ in buildings on fire, too.

c _____ take care of sick animals.

d Doctors _____ in hospitals.

e Sometimes doctors _____ far to help sick people.

5 Match the photos with the captions.

1 Police dog rests after training.

2 Boy picks up trash in the park.

3 Firefighter saves cat trapped in tree.

4 Boy plants a tree.

Comparative Forms of Short Adjectives

Real-life heroes are braver than fantasy heroes.
Elephants are bigger than many other animals.

1 **Color the matching boxes.**

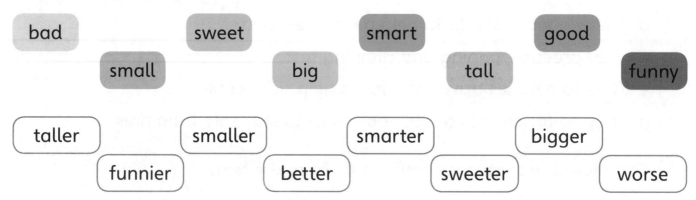

bad   sweet   smart   good

small   big   tall   funny

taller   smaller   smarter   bigger

funnier   better   sweeter   worse

2 **Circle the adjectives.**

a Cathy is **taller / shorter** than Kenny.

b Kenny is **stronger / thinner** than Cathy.

c Cathy's hair is **shorter / longer** than Kenny's.

d Cathy is **happier / sadder** than Kenny.

e Kenny is **taller / shorter** than Cathy.

f Cathy is **slower / faster** than Kenny.

3 **Look and complete the sentences.**

dog – cat   bike – train   firefighter – doctor   red – blue   park – lake

a

b

c

The _____ truck is bigger than the _____ truck.

The _____ is heavier than the _____ .

The _____ looks worse than the _____ .

d

The _____ is shorter than the _____ .

e

The _____ is faster than the _____ .

4 **Write sentences.**

a

Betty / tall / brother

_____
_____

b

Raul / slow / sister

_____
_____

c

green boots / big / red boots

_____
_____

d

hare / fast / turtle

_____
_____

My Life

Compare yourself with a friend.

1 I am shorter than _____ .

2 I am taller than _____ .

3 _____ is funnier than I am.

4 _____ is faster than I am.

1 **Read and circle *b*, *v*, and *f*. Then, number the pictures.**

1 Fred is a funny farmer who wants to be a firefighter.

2 Buddy Brown's a good player and a good basketball bouncer.

3 Two brave heroes are Vince and Viktor and they can make our lives better!

2 **Read and cross out X the word with the different initial sound.**

a friend   Fred   vet   c bouncer brown fire

b fly   Veronica   fix   d big   very   Vicky

3 **Write *b*, *v*, or *f*.**

 ___ e n c e

 ___ e e

 ___ e t

 ___ o x

 ___ a r m e r

---

1 **Read and color 🙂 or 🙁.**

a Lisa is confident. 🙂 🙁

b She isn't making eye contact. 🙂 🙁

c She is speaking clearly. 🙂 🙁

d She isn't looking up at the audience. 🙂 🙁

Improve Your Writing: Conjunctions

A conjunction joins two sentences together.
Use **and** to join two similar ideas:
This is my grandmother, and she is very special.
Use **but** to join two contrasting ideas:
She is a chef, but she doesn't work in a restaurant.

1 Read the personal narrative. Circle *and* and *but*.

A Hero in My Family

This is my grandmother, and she is very special. Grandma is a little old, but she is very healthy. She is very generous, and she does lots of things for me. She helps me with my homework, and she reads me stories. My grandmother is caring, and she is brave, too. One day there was a fire in our neighborhood, but she wasn't scared! She called the firefighters. I want to be a hero like Grandma!

2 Write S (similar ideas) or C (contrasting ideas.)

a This is my grandmother, and she is very special. ___

b Grandma is a little old, but she is very healthy. ___

c She is very generous, and she does lots of things for me. ___

d My grandmother is caring, and she is brave, too. ___

e One day there was a fire in our neighborhood, but she wasn't scared! ___

3 Read and write *and* or *but*.

a That man is blind, _____ his guide dog can see.

b Doctors are caring, _____ they are helpful, too.

c Some disabled people can't walk, _____ they can play basketball.

d Some animals are smart, _____ they can help humans.

1 READ **Look at the personal narrative on SB page 169. Circle.**

(title) (conclusion) (writer's feelings)

> ## My Personal Hero
>
> My grandpa lives with us, and I spend a lot of time with him. Grandpa is a teacher, and he works very hard every day. He likes to teach adults to read. He does not get paid for this work, but it makes him happy. He does it to help people. I am really proud of him!
>
> When Grandpa comes home in the afternoon, he helps me with my homework. Then, we go to the park, and we play on the swings. When we come back home, we play video games. My grandfather is old, but he has a lot of energy!
>
> My grandpa is my personal hero! He's a generous person, and he's also very kind. I want to be like him when I grow up!

2 **Circle Yes or No.**

a The narrative includes personal experiences.   **Yes / No**

b The narrative talks about someone the writer doesn't know.   **Yes / No**

c The writer says how he feels about his hero.   **Yes / No**

3 PLAN **Who is your personal hero? Complete the table.**

Name of Personal Hero	Experiences I Have with My Hero	How I Feel About My Hero
_____	_____	_____

4 WRITE **Complete and write a narrative about your personal hero.**

Title _____

_____

Conclusion _____

5 EDIT **Check ✓.**

WRITING CHECKLIST

☐ I included personal experiences and feelings.

☐ I included a title and a conclusion.

Ready to Read: Fiction

1 **Key Words 4** **Unscramble and write the words.**

chyit   sehiv   gicllera acreiont   rabletec   meregenyc   wslle

a

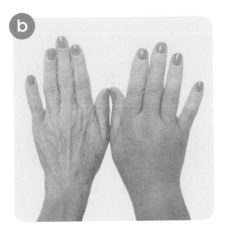

b

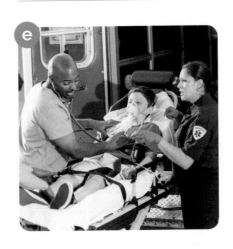

c

d

e

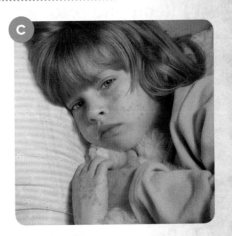

f

2 **Use words from Activity I to complete the sentences.**

There was an 1_____ at school. At lunchtime, Sibeli felt bad. She had an 2_____ reaction to something in her lunch. Her mouth began to 3_____. It looked enormous. Her teacher called an ambulance. The paramedics arrived soon, and they took Sibeli to the hospital. She is there now. She has 4_____. Her arms were 5_____ at first, but she feels better now.

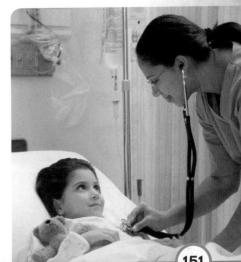

Reading Strategy: Predicting from Titles

The title of a story can give you clues about what the story is about.

1 **Read and color what the stories will be about.**

Real-life Heroes

Nurses are Heroes

2 **Read the story.**

Osman's Allergy

I'm better than all the other heroes. I'm the strongest and fastest superhero!

Osman is a superhero. His superhero suit is red and yellow—those are his favorite colors! Osman is strong, and he can fly. He flies really fast over cities and mountains.

Osman has a problem. He's allergic to bees, and there's a bee chasing him! Osman can fly fast, but the bee is faster.

Oh, no! Don't do it! That's not funny!

Osman is having an allergic reaction! His finger is swelling. It's itchy, too.

I have a gigantic red finger! This is an emergency! Please help me!

Osman is really scared now.

A young doctor helps Osman. He gives Osman an injection. Ouch!

How's your finger? Is it better?

Yes, it is better, and it's not itchy! Thank you! You're my new personal hero!

(3) Read and circle *Yes* or *No*.

a Osman is a superhero   **Yes   No**

b He can fly.   **Yes   No**

c He's slow.   **Yes   No**

d Osman is allergic to fish.   **Yes   No**

e A snake bites Osman.   **Yes   No**

f Osman's finger swells.   **Yes   No**

g Osman has a new personal hero.   **Yes   No**

(4) Complete the sentences.

> scared   heroes   happy   allergic   help

a Osman is _____ to bees.

b A bee stings Osman. He is _____.

c He needs _____ and goes to the doctor.

d Now Osman is _____.

e He knows there are other _____.

(5) Read the titles. Then circle your predictions.

1   **It's an Emergency!**

2   **Let's Help!**

a The story is about what to do when there an accident.

b The story is about what to do when there is a party.

a The story is about children who play games and have fun.

b The story is about children who are generous.

Superlative Forms of Short Adjectives

My friend is **the tallest** student in my class.
My teacher is **the funniest** person in the world.

1 Color the matching boxes.

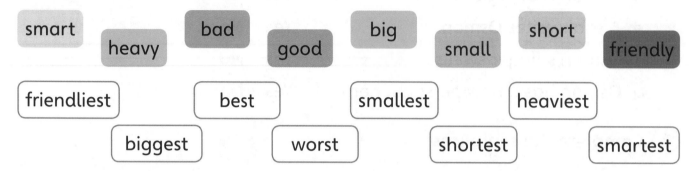

smart   heavy   bad   good   big   small   short   friendly

friendliest   best   smallest   heaviest

biggest   worst   shortest   smartest

2 Look and circle the pictures.

a

b

c

It's the biggest box.   It's the smallest marble.   It's the tallest plant.

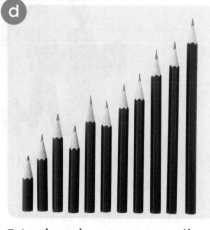

d

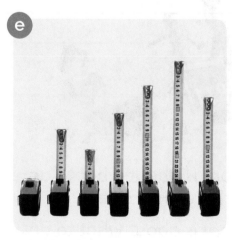

e

It's the shortest pencil.   It's the longest.

154

3 Read and circle the correct words.

The **whale / turtle** is the biggest.

The **rabbit / snail** is the fastest.

Grandma / Dad is the oldest.

The **juice / cupcake** is the sweetest.

The **boy / girl** is the happiest.

4 Write sentences with superlative adjectives.

1

small   big

2

tall   short

a _____

b _____

c _____

d _____

My Life

Write sentences about yourself and your family.

1 toy: _____ is the best.

2 person: _____ is the funniest.

3 person: _____ is the oldest.

1 **What do real-life heroes do? Mark ✓.**

a

b

c

d

e

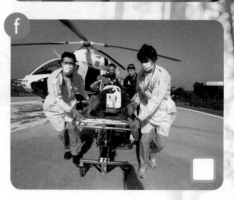
f

2 **Color a real-life hero's good actions.**

rescue people in danger

jump to a cloud

help disabled people

fly in the sky

save trapped animals

put out a fire

travel in time

help sick children

3 **Are you brave? Draw yourself.**

156

Check Your Oracy!

Read and circle *Yes* or *No*.

1 I looked up at the audience.   **Yes / No**

2 I made eye contact.   **Yes / No**

3 I spoke clearly and at the right pace.   **Yes / No**

How can we talk about heroes?

The Big Challenge

(1) Color 😊 or 🙁 .

| José Andrés | Mahatma Gandhi | Greta Thunberg |

I did research on world heroes and chose one.   😊 🙁

I drew a picture on a piece of white posterboard.   😊 🙁

I wrote information about the person.   😊 🙁

I presented my hero to the class.   😊 🙁

The Big Question and **Me**

Think and mark ✓. In Unit 8, I learned …

☐ a to talk about real-life heroes.

☐ b that bravery is important.

☐ c that we can do small things at home to be heroes.

(1) Complete the sentences.

> generous   helpful   caring   blind   brave

a _____ people act lovingly to others.

b A _____ boy likes helping his friends.

c _____ heroes are not scared.

d A _____ girl likes giving.

e Special dogs help _____ people.

(2) Unscramble and write the words.

a  rabecetl

_____

b  ihesv

_____

c  mereengyc

_____

d  eahvy

_____

e  eahthyl

_____

(3) Read and match to complete the sentences.

1 Wild animals live in the

2 Animals help people who are

3 Hives make your skin

4 Trained dogs can identify different

5 Depressed people need

☐ a itchy.

☐ b scents.

☐ c wilderness.

☐ d affection.

☐ e disabled.

8

④ Form comparative adjectives to complete the sentences.

a | fast | A rabbit is _____ than a snail.

b | long | A snake is _____ than an earthworm.

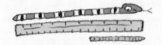

c | heavy | An elephant is _____ than a panda.

d | slow | Turtles are _____ than sharks.

e | small | A mouse is _____ than a cat.

⑤ Write the words. Then answer.

a (funny) Who's the _____ hero? _Omar_

b (thin) Who's the _____ hero? _____

c (tall) Who's the _____ hero? _____

d (short) Who's the _____ hero? _____

e (strong) Who's _____ hero? _____

Kira   Vicky   Omar

⑥ Circle the correct conjunction.

a Superheroes are stronger than doctors, **and / but** doctors are real-life heroes.

b Firefighters are brave, **and / but** they can put out fires and rescue people.

c Animal heroes can't speak, **and / but** they are really smart.

d Nurses are helpful, **and / but** they take care of sick people.

1 **Look and number.**

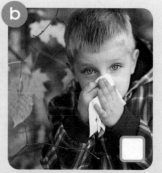

1 car accident

2 cat in a tree

3 fire

4 allergic reaction

5 snake bite

2 **Match the questions and answers.**

1 What's your name?

2 What's the problem?

3 What's your address?

4 What's your telephone number?

☐ (554) 934-6289.

☐ 123 Apple Street.

☐ A building is on fire.

☐ Tara.

3 **Number the dialogue lines in order.**

☐ What's the problem?

☐ Please hurry!

☐ Don't worry! We'll help you!

☐ There's an emergency!

☐ My cousin is having an allergic reaction to a plant.

☐1 911. How can I help you?

What can you remember about ... Unit 8?

① Circle.

A **blind** / **smart** person can't see.

② Unscramble and write the words.

A hero is gneeousr _____

and ingcar _____

③ What is this?

_____

④ Complete the sentence.

My head is i_____ .

⑤ Circle the correct picture.

wilderness

⑥ Circle the words that have the same initial sound as *fire*.

fly   Vicky   fall

⑦ Complete the word.

e m __ r g e __ c __

⑧ Circle the correct word.

A whale is **bigger** / **biggest** than a lion.

⑨ Circle the correct name.

Cesar / Devin / Brie has an allergic reaction.

⑩ Unscramble the sentence.

Who's / hero / the / real-life / best / ?

_____

Check your answers in the Student's Book. How did you do?

7–10 ☐ **Great!**   **4–6** ☐ **Good!**   **0–3** ☐ **Try harder!**

? 😃 What is a hero?

A hero is helpful, caring, g_____ s, and brave.

9 How do inventions change our lives?

1 ▶ 9.1 **Watch the video. Complete the graphic organizer.**

England toothbrush India bicycle
China computer 1800s 1970s wheel

Invention	Where?	When?
shampoo	_____	1500s
_____	_____	600 years ago
_____		Stone Age
modern _____	_____	1885
first metal ship		_____
first personal _____		_____

2 **Key Words 1** **Number the inventions. Then, write the words.**

1 It was invented in China.

2 The first one was as big as a room.

3 It helps a vehicle to move.

4 It was invented in England.

5 It's bigger than a boat.

a ☐   b ☐   c ☐

d ☐   e ☐

Ready to Read: Nonfiction

1 Key Words 2 **Circle the letters and write the words.**

a

i a n u v e s n b r t o s r

_____

b

p s r i m n t i j n g w p r a e c s s

_____

c

t e o a w s d t e h r

_____

d

t e o l o e d s c u o b p a e

_____

e

h e o u a b t

_____

f

c m h e u w e i v n j g q g o u m

_____

g

c m o e t d t o v n j c q a o n d i y

_____

2 **For each sentence write a word from Activity I.**

a It makes bread warm and brown: _____

b It's used to look at the stars: _____

c In the past, people used it to make books: _____

d This is someone who makes new things: _____

e It's candy that you can chew: _____

f It's soft candy that is made with sugar: _____

g Fire and the sun do this: _____

Reading Strategy: Fact or Opinion

A fact is something you can prove is true. An opinion is what you think.

(1) Underline the facts and the opinions.

fact ~~~~~~~~   opinion ~~~~~~~~

Alexander Graham Bell was an inventor.

He made the telephone.

The telephone is a great invention.

It was invented in 1876.

Old telephones are boring.

(2) Read the text.

Inventions

The telephone, the telescope, and the microscope are three inventions that changed people's lives.

The Telescope

In 1609 Galileo Galilei made a telescope. He pointed it to the sky and looked at the moon and stars. He discovered the rings of Saturn and the moons of Jupiter, too. Then, he found that Earth and other planets traveled around the sun. Galileo's telescope was the best invention at the time. Today, some modern telescopes are really big.

The Rings of Saturn
v

The Moons of Jupiter >

The Telephone

Alexander Graham Bell invented the telephone in 1876. Many years ago, telephone signals traveled through cables. Modern telephones don't have any cables. Now, we have cell phones that work as computers and cameras. Cell phones are amazing!

The Microscope

Hans and Zacharias Janssen made a microscope in Holland in the 1590s. This invention helped scientists to study very small living things. Today, doctors and scientists use microscopes at hospitals. They use them to find the cause of sickness. The microscope is the greatest invention of all time.

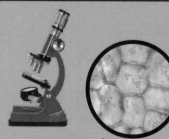
Plant Under a Microscope

3 Write *F* for fact and *O* for opinion.

a The telephone was an important invention. _____

b It was invented by Alexander Graham Bell in 1876. _____

c Some modern telescopes are very big. _____

d Galileo's telescope was the best invention at the time. _____

e Hans and Zacharias Janssen made a microscope in Holland in the 1590s. _____

f The microscope is the greatest invention of all time. _____

g This invention helped scientists to study very small living things. _____

4 Match the sentence parts.

1 Galileo

2 He

3 Years ago, telephone signals

4 Now cell phones

5 The telephone was invented

6 Hans and Zacharias Janssen

7 Doctors and scientists

☐ a by Alexander Graham Bell.

☐ b don't have cables.

☐ c made a telescope.

☐ d discovered the rings of Saturn.

☐ e traveled through cables.

☐ f use microscopes.

☐ g made a microscope.

5 Write a fact and an opinion about each invention.

cotton candy

sugar   delicious

Fact: It has sugar.

Opinion: _____

toaster

heats   important

Fact: _____

Opinion: _____

Grammar in Context

Should for Recommendations

You **should use** the toaster carefully. ✓
You **shouldn't eat** too much cotton candy. ✗

What should I do to be healthy?

① **Circle the correct recommendations.**

a You should change your toothbrush.   You shouldn't change your toothbrush.

b You should eat burnt food.   You shouldn't eat burnt food.

c You should exercise.   You shouldn't exercise.

d You should eat vegetables.   You shouldn't eat vegetables.

e You should eat a lot of sugar.   You shouldn't eat a lot of sugar.

② **Match the pictures to the recommendations.**

a ☐ You shouldn't eat all that food.

b ☐ You should recycle plastic.

c ☐ You should help with the chores at home.

d ☐ You shouldn't throw garbage on the beach.

e ☐ You should plant trees.

3 Complete the sentences with *should* or *shouldn't*.

1 You _____ draw on the wall.

2 You _____ turn off the computer.

3 You _____ leave that chocolate bar on the table.

4 You _____ make your bed.

5 You _____ pick up your toy cars.

4 Write sentences with *should* or *shouldn't*.

exercise

_____

eat all those cupcakes

_____

eat healthy food

_____

leave garbage on the beach

_____

My Life

Make recommendations to someone in your family.

Dear _____ ,

You should _____ .

You shouldn't _____ .

(1) Read and number the pictures.

1 Three birds, three birds,
hear some loud thunder.

2 Three birds, three birds,
that are baby, mother,
and father.

3 Three birds, three birds,
baby, mother, and father,
throw each other a feather
as they play all together.

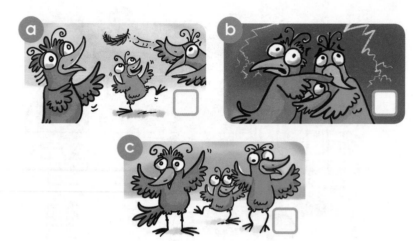

(2) Read the text in Activity I again and circle the words with _th_.

(3) Cross out X the word with the different _th_ sound.

a **th**ink	**th**ree	**th**ey
b toge**th**er	fea**th**er	**th**row
c **th**under	fa**th**er	mo**th**er
d **th**ree	**th**row	fea**th**er

(4) Write the words.

> they   throw   feather   thunder   three   mother

th as in **th**ink   **th** as in **th**e

_____   _____

_____   _____

_____   _____

---

(1) Circle the expressions for sequencing information.

I agree   (First)   Then   I don't agree.

Good job!   Next   I think   Finally

Improve Your Writing: Add -ed to Show Past Actions

With regular verbs, add -ed to show that the action happened in the past.
start + ed = started   cry + ed = cried
use + ed = used   stop + ed = stopped

(1) Read the informational text. Circle the regular verbs in the past tense.

An Invention on Wheels

Over one hundred years ago, inventors built different kinds of cars.
First, they invented electric cars. In the 1860s, these cars were
popular. Then, they made cars that used batteries, but in 1886, an
inventor named Karl Benz invented the first car that used gasoline.
Karl Benz's car had only three wheels. People liked it, and it was
more popular than electric cars. In 1908, Henry Ford built the
Model T car. It had four wheels. Most people liked it, and many
families bought them. Finally, in 2018—more than one hundred
years later—electric cars started to become popular again.

(2) Write the past form of each verb.

a plan   _planned_

b play   _____

c want   _____

d cry   _____

e invent   _____

f try   _____

(3) Complete the sentences with the past form of the verbs.

> use   help   look   recycle   worked   stop

a Galileo _____ at the moon and stars with his telescope.

b The first TVs looked like boxes, and they _____ an antenna.

c They _____ at the stop sign.

d My older brother _____ at the museum last summer.

e We _____ all our plastic bottles last weekend.

f I _____ my parents clean the kitchen yesterday.

1 READ Look at the informational text on SB page 191. Underline three facts.

2 Circle.

- inventor
- invention
- when

An Amazing Invention!

The television, or TV, is an amazing invention. Televisions receive signals, which they turn into sounds and pictures on a screen. Many inventors around the world worked to create the television.

At first, the images on TVs were black and white. In 1941, a Mexican inventor, Guillermo González Camarena, invented the color TV.

The first TV sets looked like boxes, and they used an antenna. The antenna received the signal. Today, televisions are flatter and receive a digital signal.

Guillermo González Camarena

3 PLAN Think of an invention or discovery. Answer the questions about it.

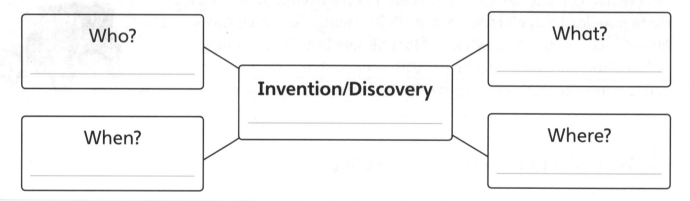

Who? _____

What? _____

Invention/Discovery _____

When? _____

Where? _____

4 WRITE Write an informational text about your invention or discovery.

_____

_____

_____

_____

5 EDIT Check ✓.

WRITING CHECKLIST

☐ I included facts about an invention or discovery.

☐ I included who invented it and when and where.

☐ I used regular past tense verbs.

1 Key Words 4 **Complete the puzzle.**

1

2

3

4

5

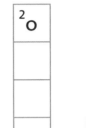
6

Crossword:

Across:
4. w _ _ t _ e r
5. k _ o c k _ o _ e

Down:
1. p r e d i c t
2. o _ e r _ a t i _ n
3. a
6. w n

2 **Use words from Activity I to complete the sentences.**

a Some scientists can _____ the _____. They can tell if it will be hot or cold, rainy or sunny.

b They can do it through _____ of the world.

c My family and I _____ two cats as pets.

d Our cats sometimes _____ things _____.

e Look! They knocked over that big _____!

Reading Strategy: Understanding the Meaning of Words in Context

Some words in a sentence or paragraph can help you understand the meaning of a new word.

1 **Read and circle the correct picture.**

The sewing machine was invented in England in 1790. The invention of the sewing machine helped people make clothes faster.

This is a sewing machine:

2 **Read the story.**

Azra's Birthday Present

Azra wants to be an **astronaut**. In her dreams, she travels to space on a big **spaceship**. In space, her mission is to collect stardust.

 Azra puts the stardust in a jar. Then, she brings it back home. The stardust **sparkles** in the jar.

In her dreams, Azra has a telescope. She uses the telescope to watch the moon and the stars. She can see some planets, too. Tomorrow is Azra's birthday. Azra predicts rain because there are some dark clouds in the sky.

The next morning, when Azra wakes up, she knows she had a dream. It's raining but she goes to the backyard. There's a big telescope in the middle of the yard.

 Azra is excited! That's the telescope she dreamed of! Azra asks her grandfather, "May I use it, Grandpa?" Azra's grandfather says happily, "Sure! It's yours! This telescope is your birthday present!"

Azra is **thrilled**! She is so happy that she jumps until she knocks over her birthday cake!

SB pages 193–98

3 **Write D for dream or R for reality.**

a Azra wants to be an astronaut.   _____

b She travels on a spaceship.   _____

c She collects stardust.   _____

d Stardust sparkles in a jar.   _____

e It's Azra's birthday.   _____

f She gets an amazing birthday present.   _____

4 **Read and complete the sentences.**

> telescope   jar   rains   dreams   collects

a In her _____ , Azra is an astronaut.

b She _____ stardust in space.

c She puts it in a _____ .

d It _____ on Azra's birthday.

e She gets a _____ as a present.

5 **Circle the blue words in the text. Then, match them with the definitions.**

1 spaceship   ☐ a someone who travels to space

2 sparkles   ☐ b very happy

3 thrilled   ☐ c a vehicle to travel in space

4 astronaut   ☐ d shines brightly

6 **Complete the text with the words from Activity 5.**

Hugo is an 1_____ from Spain. He works on space missions. He travels to Earth in a 2_____ . It is a yellow spaceship that 3_____ in the dark. Hugo has many friends on Earth. He's 4_____ to visit them on every journey.

May and *Can* for Permission

May I use a crayon? Yes, you **may**. **No, you may not.**
Can **he bring his pet?** Yes, he **can**. **No, he can't.**

(1) **Number the answers.**

1 May I use the computer?
2 Can my cat sleep in the garden?
3 May we ride our bikes?
4 Can he chew gum?
5 May I buy some cotton candy?

☐ a Yes, it can. It can play, too.
☐ b No, you may not. She's using it.
☐ c No, he can't. He's in class.
☐ d Yes, you may, but wear your helmets.
☐ e Yes, you may, but don't eat it all.

(2) **Look and circle the correct word groups.**

a May I   read that book?   write the answer?

b May we   use that chair?   take those crayons?

c Can he   open the window?   come in?

d May I   play with that ball?   ride that bike?

e Can she   take my schoolbag?   use my notebook?

3) Unscramble and write the questions.

a

we / Can / go / on that Ferris wheel / ?

_____

b

I / May / that horse / ride / ?

_____

c

Can / on the slides / play / he / ?

_____

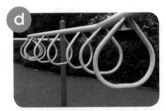

d

to the monkey bars / I / go / May / ?

_____

4) Complete the questions and the answers.

a 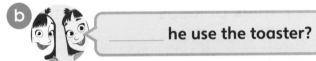 _____ I have some cotton candy?

_____ , you may.

b _____ he use the toaster?

_____ , he can't.

c May we ride our bikes in the park?

No, you _____ .

d _____ I chew gum?

Yes, you can.

My Life

How do you ask for permission?

the tablet?   with that ball?   my bike?

1 **What can you do to be an inventor? Mark ✓.**

2 **Color what curious children do.**

| think of ideas | forget about projects | feel bored | read books |

| do experiments | do homework | fight with friends | work hard |

| observe nature | ask questions | find solutions | write ideas down |

3 **Do you want to be an inventor? Draw yourself.**

Check Your Oracy!

Read and circle *Yes* or *No*.

1 We organized our routine and presented it in order. **Yes / No**
2 We used sequence words. **Yes / No**
3 The class followed our routine. **Yes / No**

The Big Challenge

How can we recognize the importance of inventions?

1 **Color** ☺ **or** ☹ .

We brainstormed important inventions.	☺	☹
We made a list of the three most important inventions.	☺	☹
We made a chart.	☺	☹
We drew a picture of each invention and wrote about the reason we cannot live without it.	☺	☹
We presented our chart to the class.	☺	☹

The Big Question and Me

Think and mark ✓. In Unit 9, I learned …

- [ ] a to talk about why inventions are important.
- [ ] b that curiosity helps us to become inventors.
- [ ] c to talk about inventions that changed the world.

1 **Write the inventions in alphabetical order.**

bicycle   telescope   wheel   ship   computer   toaster

1 _____   4 _____

2 _____   5 _____

3 _____   6 _____

2 **Match the sentences with the pictures. Then, write the words.**

ship   shampoo   flight   printing press   toaster   inventor

a ☐

b ☐

1 You wash your hair with it.

2 This person creates new things.

3 It was used to make books.

4 It can carry things over the ocean.

5 It heats bread and makes it brown.

6 This is a journey in the air.

c ☐

d ☐

e ☐

f ☐

3 **Complete the sentences.**

burnt   melt   knock over   weather   observation

a _____ helps some people to predict the _____.

b Don't put your ice cream in the sun, or it will _____.

c That cat will _____ my jar.

d I didn't eat the _____ toast from the toaster.

9

4 **Circle *should* or *shouldn't*.**

 **a** You **should / shouldn't** leave garbage in the street.

 **b** You **should / shouldn't** eat healthy food.

 **c** You **should / shouldn't** exercise.

 **d** You **should / shouldn't** eat so much sugar.

 **e** You **should / shouldn't** recycle paper.

5 **Complete the questions or the answers.**

 **a**

 **b**

 **c**

 **d**

May I ride my bike?

Yes, _____.

_____ she play with her pet?

Yes, she can.

_____ we play in the living room?

No, you may not.

Can I buy some chewing gum?

No, _____.

6 **Write the sentences in the past.**

a Gael **wants** to be an inventor.

_____

b He **tries** to make new things.

_____

c He **plans** interesting projects.

_____

d He **changes** people's lives.

_____

(1) Look and circle. Some words might match more than one color.

| musical instruments | food | celebrations | your community |

| your neighborhood | heroes | inventions |

firefighter   trumpet   generous   nurse

cake   doctor   violin   brave

printing press   watermelon   computer   party

present   hospital   carrots

(2) Match.

1 I ask questions.   ☐ a My audience can understand what I say.

2 I make eye contact.   ☐ b I use these words: *First, Next, Then, Finally.*

3 I sequence my information.   ☐ c I want to learn more.

4 I speak clearly and at the right pace.   ☐ d I look at my audience.

(3) Write sequencing words on the lines.

Finally   First   ~~Next~~   Then

We spoke about inventions.

_____, we talked about the train.

___Next___, we described the first plane.

_____, my classmates showed pictures of different cars.

_____, I drew a picture of my favorite invention.

What can you remember about ... Unit 9?

① Circle the correct word.

Burnt / Melted bread is dark brown.

② Unscramble the words and complete the sentence.

serboaviont   direpct

Careful _____ helps scientists _____ the weather.

③ How many wheels are there?

_____

④ Unscramble the question.

we / May / an invention / talk about / ?

_____

⑤ Circle the correct picture.

chewing gum

⑥ Which words have the same sound as *thunder*?

three   father   thirty

⑦ Complete the word.

t __ l __ s c __ __ e

⑧ Circle the correct words.

You **should / shouldn't** work hard.

You **should / shouldn't** feel bored.

⑨ What color was Fluffy at the beginning of the story?

_____

⑩ Complete the answer.

Can he walk his dog in the park? Yes, he _____.

Check your answers in the Student's Book. How did you do?
7–10 ☐ Great!   4–6 ☐ Good!   0–3 ☐ Try harder!

? 😃 How do inventions change our lives?

Inventions make our lives **easier / harder**.

All About Oracy!

Unit 1: Ground Rules for Discussions

Ground rules help us discuss things more effectively.

1 That's important.

2 That's not important.

Unit 2: Giving Positive Feedback

We can give positive feedback when people share their ideas or work.

3 Great job!

4 That's awesome!

Unit 3: Giving Opinions

When somebody gives an opinion, you can agree or disagree. It is important to be respectful.

I think sugar is bad.

5 I think ...

6 I agree.

7 I disagree

Unit 4: Asking Questions for Clarification

When we don't understand something, it helps to ask questions.

Some stingrays swam next to me.

What's a stingray?

8 I don't understand.

9 Can you repeat that?

10 What's a/an X?

Unit 5: Participating in a Discussion

When we participate in a discussion, it's important to give suggestions.

11 Lets ...

12 How about ...?

Unit 6: Giving an Explanation

You can explain things better by giving reasons.

I think we should bring burgers and fries. What do you think, Jack?

Well, I disagree because …

13 (Why?)
Because …

Unit 7: Speaking Clearly at the Right Pace

When you give a presentation, it is important to speak clearly and not too fast.

14 Can you speak more slowly?

15 Can you speak up?

Unit 8: Speaking in Front of an Audience

When we speak in front of an audience, it is important to look up and make eye contact.

16 Look at this …

17 This is …

Unit 9: Sequencing Information

When you give a presentation, it is important to organize the information and put it in order.

18 First,

19 Next,

20 Then,

21 Finally,

Acknowledgments

The authors and publishers acknowledge the following sources of copyright material and are grateful for the permissions granted. While every effort has been made, it has not always been possible to identify the sources of all the material used or to trace all copyright holders. If any omissions are brought to our notice, we will be happy to include the appropriate acknowledgments on reprinting and in the next update to the digital edition, as applicable.

Key: U = Unit.

Photography

The following images are sourced from Getty Images.

UI: Antenna/fStop; Martin Appleson/Moment; Grant Faint/Photographer's Choice RF; JodiJacobson/E+; Caiaimage/Agnieszka Olek/Caiaimage; Jihyun Seo/EyeEm; Jonatan Fernstrom/Cultura; Robert Kneschke/EyeEm; skodonnell/E+; Johner Images; Ragnvid, Magnus; stockcam/E+; Nikada/E+; Caiaimage/Trevor Adeline; Fuse/Corbis; lissart/E+; JGI/Jamie Grill; kali9/E+; Jacky Parker Photography/Moment; Image Source/DigitalVision; susan.k/Moment; miodrag ignjatovic/E+; Elke Meitzel/Cultura; Lee Williams/Moment; Tony Garcia/Photodisc; Alexander Spatari/Moment; ChuckSchugPhotography/E+; Pulse/Corbis; Keith Brofsky/UpperCut Images; fanjianhua/Moment; J614/DigitalVision Vectors; fitopardo.com/Moment; Tomekbudujedomek/Moment; DNY59/E+; Creative Crop/Photodisc; CactuSoup/E+; YinYang/iStock/Getty Images Plus; David Miller/EyeEm; Maurice Rivera/EyeEm; Aliraza Khatri's Photography/Moment; John Giustina/The Image Bank; David Crespo/Moment; tuncaycetin/E+; Richard Newstead/Moment; U2: Fuse/Corbis; Vstock LLC/Vstock; yasinguneysu/E+; aydinmutlu/E+; David Freund/Photodisc; Westend61; xavierarnau/E+; Jose Luis Pelaez Inc/DigitalVision; Mike Powell/Stone; Diane Labombarbe/DigitalVision Vectors; JGI/Jamie Grill; ImagesBazaar/Brand X Pictures; annapekunova/RooM; Pan Hong/Moment; Andre Vogelaere/Moment; Pete Saloutos; Ariel Skelley/DigitalVision; Funwithfood/E+; kali9/E+; Westend61; Zero Creatives/Image Source; Granger Wootz; mother image/Photodisc; rubberball; Stockbyte; Mark Edward Atkinson; MIXA; Niedring/Drentwett/MITO images; Alexandra Jursova/Moment Open; Steve Debenport/E+; delalidela/iStock/Getty Images Plus; Synergee/E+; koya79/iStock/Getty Images Plus; Classen Rafael/EyeEm; Axel Bueckert/EyeEm; nkbimages/E+; Chee Siong Teh/EyeEm; Banar Fil Ardhi/EyeEm; dlerick/E+; Akepong Srichaichana/EyeEm; RuthBlack/iStock /Getty Images Plus; U3: Caziopeia/E+; TheCrimsonMonkey/E+; carlosgaw/E+; Nredmond/E+; Akepong Srichaichana/EyeEm; Nattawut Lakjit/EyeEm; Nathan ALLIARD/Photononstop/Getty Images Plus; Science Photo Library; Image Source/DigitalVision; pbombaert/Moment; R.Tsubin/Moment; moi/a.collectionRF; Rico K_dder/EyeEm; Floortje/E+; Pedro Mariscal/EyeEm; Manjurul Haque/EyeEm; Ray Kachatorian; burwellphotography/E+; Westend61; melecis/iStock/Getty Images Plus; Yevgen Romanenko/Moment; FotografiaBasica/E+; Foodcollection; ValentynVolkov/iStock/Getty Images Plus; laartist/E+; Hero Images; Jonathan Kitchen/Photodisc; fcafotodigital/E+; Andrzej Siwiec/EyeEm; Marilyn Nieves/E+; Ruth Bushi/EyeEm; Adam Gault/OJO Images; RedHelga/E+; DebbiSmirnoff/E+; Classen Rafael/EyeEm; Creativ Studio Heinemann; Natthakan Jommanee/EyeEm; ASIFE/iStock/Getty Images Plus; Spencer Jones/Photolibrary; I550539/iStock/Getty Images Plus; Dmytro/iStock/Getty Images Plus; Douglas Sacha/Moment; domnicky/iStock/Getty Images Plus; RuthBlack/iStock/Getty Images Plus; Skathi/iStock/Getty Images Plus; Lauren Burke/DigitalVision; Juan Jose Lopez Brotons/EyeEm; gerenme/E+; hsvrs/E+; Janet Moore/EyeEm; Jose Luis Pelaez Inc/DigitalVision; Neyya/E+; hdere/E+; PixelBay/E+; PixelBay/iStock/Getty Images Plus; ktmoffitt/iStock/Getty Images Plus; tacojim/E+; Richard Coombs/EyeEm; Copyright Xinzheng. All Rights Reserved/Moment; Toson Rueangsuksut/EyeEm; huePhotography/E+; Ariel Skelley/DigitalVision; uniquely india; Tom Merton/Caiaimage; natthanim/iStock/Getty Images Plus; rubberball; carlosgaw/E+; Didier Gabiam/EyeEm; Diana Sayson/EyeEm; Mohd Fildraus Halimi/EyeEm; C Squared Studios/Photodisc; LauriPatterson/iStock/Getty Images Plus; ithinksky/E+; Nora Carol Photography/Moment; milanfoto/E+; Vesna Jovanovic/EyeEm; Rermrat Kaewpukdee/EyeEm; Dimitris66/E+; deepblue4you/iStock/Getty Images Plus; Poh Kim Yeoh/EyeEm; pixelfit/E+; Image Source; Samere Fahim Photography/Moment; subjug/E+; U4: Marco Bottigelli/Moment; Yustinus/RooM; Patrick Thangsombat/Moment; Anton Petrus/Moment; James O'Neil/DigitalVision; Sebastián Crespo Photography/Moment; Joe Carini/Perspectives/Getty Images Plus; abile/E+; Donghun Jeon/Moment; A. Chederros/ONOKY; SolStock/E+; InterNetwork Media/DigitalVision; Witthaya Prasongsin/Moment; dulancristian/E+; Natthawut Nungsanther/EyeEm; Dani Daniar/EyeEm; MAIKA 777/Moment Open; matooker/E+; Benjamin Wuermli/EyeEm; Wf Sihardian/EyeEm; Kate Stoupas/Moment; M Swiet Productions/Moment; Feifei Cui-Paoluzzo/Moment; Oleandra9/iStock/Getty Images Plus; Razvan Chisu/EyeEm; Holly Harris/Photodisc; travelpixpro/E+; powerofforever/E+; Photodisc; Wicki58/E+; Martin Schneider/EyeEm; Kristan Jacobsen/EyeEm; Chris Winsor/Moment; Buena Vista Images/DigitalVision; Jeff R Clow/Moment; Thinkstock/Stockbyte; Jose Luis Pelaez Inc/DigitalVision; Digital Vision; Rayman/Photodisc; VisitBritain/James McCormick; Elke Meitzel/Cultura; Garry Gay/Stockbyte; Hero Images; Wilhelm Doru Gombos/EyeEm; Roger Harris/Science Photo Library; Leonello Calvetti/Stocktrek Images; Sirachai Arunrugstichai/Moment; Image Source RF/ÂWhit Richardson; japatino/Moment; Jennifer Uppendahl/EyeEm; Guido Dingemans, De Eindredactie/Moment; Jamie Grill; secret agent mike/Moment; nicolamargaret/E+; CactuSoup/E+; Philipp Von Buttlar/EyeEm; mikroman6/Moment Open; Josie Elias/Photographer's Choice RF; Moritz Witter/EyeEm; Laetizia Haessig/EyeEm; Magda Molina/EyeEm; FEBRUARY/Moment; richardseeleyphotography.com/Moment; Westend61; Sudhir Misra/EyeEm; Shana Novak/DigitalVision; Ng Sok Lian/Moment; DSGpro/E+; Jure Gasparic/EyeEm; angela labarbera/FOAP; clu/E+; agustavop/E+; Images authentiques par le photographe gettysteph/Moment; Miriam Rodríguez Domingo/EyeEm; Hill Street Studios/DigitalVision; Matteo Colombo/DigitalVision; U5: Imgorthand/E+; Fuse/Corbis; Severin Schweiger/Cultura; Hill Street Studios; sarahwolfephotography/Moment; Jamie Garbutt/DigitalVision; scanrail/iStock/Getty Images Plus; Caiaimage/Tom Merton/OJO+; Eva Oppitz/EyeEm; MoMo Productions/DigitalVision; Khotcharak Siriwong/EyeEm; nikom khotjan/Moment; Tetra Images; C Squared Studios/Photodisc; Kativ/E+; Stockbyte; Nastasic/E+; Leonello Calvetti/Science Photo Library; Axel Bueckert/EyeEm; Philippe TURPIN/Photononstop; Digital Vision/Photodisc; Jose Luis Pelaez Inc/DigitalVision; clu/DigitalVision Vectors; pagadesign/E+; adventtr/E+; Marc Romanelli; Hill Street Studios/DigitalVision; Glow Images; Rubberball/Chris Alvanas; Alexander Sorokopud/Moment; Simon Webb & Duncan Nicholls/OJO Images; Caroline Schiff; Alyssa B. Young/Moment; imagenavi; Lebedinski/iStock/Getty Images Plus; Vermette/E+; BJI/Blue Jean Images; colematt/iStock/Getty Images Plus; MarsBars/E+; Jamie Grill/Tetra Images; Ghislain & Marie David de Lossy/Cultura; JGI/Tom Grill; Marta Nardini/Moment; Ariel Skelley/DigitalVision; ferrantraite/Vetta; JGI/Jamie Grill; damircudic/E+; U6: ronniechua/iStock Editorial/Getty Images Plus; Flavio Coelho/Moment; Buena Vista Images/DigitalVision; Enrique Díaz/7cero/Moment; loonger/E+; Jose A. Bernat Bacete/Moment; Corey Ford/Stocktrek Images; Mark Stevenson/Stocktrek Images; Daniel Eskridge/Stocktrek Images; Stocktrek Images; Alice Turner/Stocktrek Images; Leonello Calvetti/Stocktrek Images; Sciepro/Science Photo Library; Jose A. Bernat Bacete/Moment Open; Dorling Kindersley; Simon Roulstone; Roger Harris/Science Photo Library; Vladimir Liparti/EyeEm; beklaus/E+; ExperienceInteriors/E+; Marc Keller/EyeEm; buchsammy/Moment; Victor Walsh Photography/Moment; Ariel Skelley/DigitalVision; filadendron/E+; Nobumichi Tamura/Stocktrek Images; Arthur Dorety/Stocktrek Images; Elena Duvernay/Stocktrek Images; imagenavi; xefstock/iStock/Getty Images Plus; beastfromeast/DigitalVision Vectors; Ng Sok Lian/EyeEm; Alex CaoLKL/Photodisc; Punsayaporn Thaveekul/EyeEm; Chee Siong Teh/EyeEm; ryszard filipowicz/500Px Plus; Nehru Sulejmanovski/EyeEm; Michelle Arnold/EyeEm; PhotoObjects.net/Getty Images Plus; Ray Pietro/Photodisc; Pierre-Yves Babelon/Moment; Dave Williams/Moment; Ivan/Moment; Alexander Rieber/EyeEm; Sergey Krasovskiy/Stocktrek Images; Mark Garlick/Science Photo Library; U7: Mark Andersen/Photolibrary Video; Andersen Ross/Verve+; kajakiki/Creatas Video; Carol Yepes/Moment; Juanmonino/E+; Melanie Hobson/EyeEm; Kitti Boonnitrod/Moment; kickstand/E+; Image Source; Floortje/E+; Yevgen Romanenko/Moment; II7 Imagery/Moment; SJB Vision/Moment; stockcam/E+; Oleksandra Korobova/Moment; StockPhotoAstur/iStock/Getty Images Plus; Glow Images; Tatiana Kolesnikova/Moment Open; Asiaselects; Otto Stadler/Photographer's Choice RF; David Fletcher/Moment Open; gmnicholas/E+; wildestanimal/Moment; Michael Candelori/EyeEm; FatCamera/E+; Tolga TEZCAN/E+; John D. Buffington/DigitalVision; Kirbyphoto/iStock/Getty Images Plus; Carlos_bcn/iStock/Getty Images Plus; CSA Images; Noctiluxx/E+; Azirull Amin Aripin/EyeEm; rubberball; pagadesign/E+; alvarez/E+; Visage/Stockbyte; ArtMarie/E+; kali9/E+; Hill Street Studios/DigitalVision; Alistair Berg/DigitalVision; Ariel Skelley/DigitalVision; Daniel Chetroni/EyeEm; Marc Romanelli; Kittiyut Phornphibul/EyeEm; fstop123/E+; shapecharge/E+; Hidetsugu Mori/Aflo; Ivary; Rocky89/E+; Cavan Images/Cavan; Monkey Business Images/Stockbyte; Tony Garcia/Image Source; ptaxa/E+; Tom Merton/Caiaimage; Hero Images/DigitalVision; Mohd Rosli/EyeEm; Fran Polito/Moment; Mike Kemp; Luke Stanton/Moment; Anuska Sampedro/Moment; Lawrence Manning/Corbis; plimages/E+; Ragnar Schmuck/Moment; U8: kali9/E+; asiseeit/E+; Tetra Images/Brand X Pictures; FS Productions; TerryJ/E+; altrendo images/Altrendo; Chris Winsor/Moment; Martin Moxter; BrentBinghamPhotography.com/Moment; Design Pics/Con Tanasiuk; Hero Images; skynesher/E+; FatCamera/E+; jonya/E+; ParkerDeen/iStock/Getty Images Plus; J-Roman/E+; Monty Rakusen/Cultura; Dean Mitchell/E+; David Toase/Photodisc; Kathrin Auzinger-Hotzel/EyeEm; Rubberball/Mike Kemp; GoranStimac/E+; shene/Moment Open; PeopleImages/E+; Jay's photo/Moment; pixdeluxe/E+; Andrew Olney/OJO Images; Imazins; ER Productions Limited/DigitalVision; Rayman/Photodisc; seraficus/E+; BigPappa/E+; macniak/iStock/Getty Images Plus; nautilus_shell_studios/E+; Tetra Images; Vstock LLC/Vstock; Jose Luis Pelaez Inc/DigitalVision; David Malan/Photographer's Choice RF; Pulse/Corbis/Getty Images Plus; Gyro Photography/amanaimagesRF; Mehmet Hilmi Barcin/E+; Magnilion/DigitalVision Vectors; JohnnyGreig/E+; Ade_Deployed/E+; Colin Anderson Productions pty ltd/DigitalVision; JGI/Jamie Grill; sarote pruksachat/Moment; IMoreCreative/E+; Echo/Juice Images; chmuller/iStock/Getty Images Plus; PictureLake/E+; Mike Coppola/Getty Images Entertainment; Michael Campanella/Getty Images News; David Sonnweber/500px; Imgorthand/E+; Image Source; Russell Illig/Photodisc; Mark Kostich/E+; Jodie Griggs/Moment; Ashley Corbin-Teich/Image Source; duckycards/E+; Image Source/ Photodisc; Nick Brundle Photography/Moment; Alexander Spatari/Moment; BJI/Blue Jean Images; U9: alxpin/E+; DNY59/E+; DonNichols/E+; Douglas Sacha/Moment Open; Cimmerian/E+; portishead/E+; Richard Ransier/Corbis/VCG/Corbis; Valerie Loiseleux/E+; Steve Wisbauer/Stockbyte; Thinkstock Images/Stockbyte; Jasmin Merdan/Moment; Novo Images/UIG; Ryan McVay/Photodisc; Dorling Kindersley; JoKMedia/E+; Hendrik Sulaiman/EyeEm; Suriyo Hmun Kaew/EyeEm; TinaFields/E+; @Niladri Nath/Moment; Stocktrek/Stockbyte; Nnehring/E+; Pannonia/E+; ImageMediaGroup/E+; Pavlina Boralieva Photography/Moment; FatCamera/E+; altmodern/E+; Rubberball/Nicole Hill; apomares/E+; Science & Society Picture Library/SSPL; Eric Van Den Brulle/Stockbyte; shaunl/E+; Anne Stephneson/EyeEm; Westend61; Fernando Trabanco Fotografia/Moment; Paper Boat Creative/DigitalVision; Steve Shott/Dorling Kindersley; PeopleImages/E+; CollinsChin/E+; George Mdivanian/EyeEm; Matt Anderson Photography/Moment; Deyan Georgiev/500Px Plus; Ron_Thomas/E+; Hisham Ibrahim/Moment Mobile; mozcann/E+; Suwit Nimjitt/Moment; Creative Crop/Photodisc; damircudic/E+; Andersen Ross Photography Inc/DigitalVision; izusek/E+; JGI/Jamie Gril; Steve Debenport/E+; R.Creation/orion/amana images/Getty Images; Science Photo Library; Ursula Klawitter/Radius Images; hudiemm/E+; Nastasic/DigitalVision Vectors; Skathi/iStock/Getty Images Plus; Monika Nesslauer; onurdongel/E+; Stockbyte; Steve Wisbauer/Photodisc; Artur Debat/Moment.

The following photos are sourced from other sources.

U2: Courtesy of European Central Bank; U8: Courtesy of Greta Thunberg.

Illustrations

Antonio Cuesta; Beccy Blake; Beth Hughes; Dean Gray; Erin Taylor; Gema Garcia; Jimena Sanchez; Jose De Santiago; Leo Trinidad; Lisa Williams; Parwinder Singh; Sofia Cardoso. Cover illustrations by Bonnie Pang (Astound).